A Way of Seeing

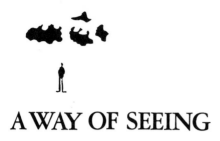

A WAY OF SEEING

A Critical Study of James Agee
by Alfred T. Barson

University of Massachusetts Press

To my Father and Mother

Contents

Many men embrace contradictions; they carry their inconsistencies with the aplomb of a Chaplin pirouette. But few men expose their inconsistencies with the savage willfulness of self-destruction. When they do, we are likely to think of them as madmen or perhaps artists. And when they die, either we honor them by calling them geniuses or dishonor them by calling them fakes. While he lived, James Agee was considered an artist and a genius. When he died, the terms remained. Surely they are nothing more or less than testimonies of faith, and perhaps it is a disservice to question faith. But in another regard we should realize that this faith has become, in some cases, superstition. The titles alone of articles about him—"A Cult Grew Around a Many-Sided Writer"; "James Agee—'Strange and Wonderful' "; "Jim Agee, A Memoir"; "Goodbye to James Agee"; "Tender Realist"; "Memories of James Agee"—proclaim more than faith. They tell of a unique individual whose talent with words was prodigious but who was a "captive of the Luce publications," who did not have the kind of "toughness and shrewdness . . . to use instead of being used," who was "incapable of taking on any kind of script or journalism and doing it with his left hand the way others could," whose talent was "too versatile" for an age of specialization, or whose country invited him to "divert his energies in a dozen different directions." [1]

Perhaps all these opinions contain some truth, but on the whole they beg a question. As John Updike has written in reviewing Agee's letters to Father James Harold Flye, they "invite us to lament over Agee's aborted and tormented career." [2] In many ways James Agee's career *was* aborted" and "tormented." Technically, he finished only two of his books—his volume of verse collected in 1934, *Permit Me Voyage,* and the novella he wrote in 1950 about his boarding-school days in Tennessee, *The Morning*

Watch. Other than commercial work, several short stories, film "sketches," and assorted poems, the remainder (including his major work as well as the manuscripts stuffed in the fabled packing box and piano bench) is unfinished. Yet no man is an artist because of what he does not do (although Agee remained "tormented" by this problem until his death); he is an artist because of what he does. And in some ways James Agee understood this fact far better than most of those who write about him. In working notes for his review of Charlie Chaplin's *Monsieur Verdoux* he claimed,

> *It cannot be defensibly insisted . . . that a ruthless society and the depth of one's love are between them responsible for evil. Their pressure is enormous . . . but whatever that pressure may be, every man is responsible for his own soul.*[3]

Updike came to a similar conclusion: no matter what pressure prevented Agee from finishing his work, the author of the best passages of *Let Us Now Praise Famous Men* and *A Death in the Family* needs no apology for his art.

Thus there is none in this book. I have attempted to identify the sources of Agee's art in his life and times and to trace its development and decline. A tactical problem, however, kept reasserting itself—the sheer size and scope of Agee's undertakings. Until the time he published *Permit Me Voyage,* he considered himself a poet. It was with the idea that he would write poetry that in 1932 he had accepted a position on the staff of *Fortune* magazine. And it was as a poet that he suffered the disillusionment of a working writer during the Great Depression. However, his journalism influenced his talent, and it was not entirely as a poet, but also as a journalist, that he accomplished the work which will stand as his masterpiece, *Let Us Now Praise Famous Men.* With photographer Walker Evans, Agee was assigned by *Fortune* to travel through the South in the summer of 1936 and to write a series of articles on sharecroppers, Southern unions, and New Deal programs. *Fortune* held the manuscript for nearly a year before they rejected it. Upon the rejection, Agee left the magazine to freelance and, with Evans, to find another publisher.

During this period—roughly 1937 to 1942—Agee more or less forgot about poetry. When he returned to the Luce organization in October 1939, it was as a book reviewer for *Time*. Shortly after the 1941 publication of *Famous Men*, he took over the "Films" department from Whittaker Chambers and began his now famous movie reviews. In November 1942 Margaret Marshall, then literary editor for *The Nation*, invited him to write another, longer column on film. By 1945, along with Chambers, he was writing "Special Projects" throughout *Time* as well as movie and book reviews, and his film column for *The Nation*. As was the case with most Americans, however, the war and its aftermath exacted its toll from him. He was horrified by the atomic bombings of Hiroshima and Nagasaki, profoundly affected when his friend Chambers put the nation on trial by announcing that he and others had operated as Russian agents in Washington during the 1930s. In reaction, Agee retreated to a more personal means of expression, first by film satire, then by finally breaking with *Time* in 1948 to write a novel concerning the death of his father. The four years between 1947 and 1951 mark his most creative period. After his film satire "Dedication Day," published in 1946, Agee launched two major pieces—another film satire to star Charlie Chaplin and later entitled "Scientists and Tramps" and his posthumously published novel, *A Death in the Family*. He also finished writing dialogue for *The Quiet One*, a documentary film released in 1948; two essays for *Life*, "Comedy's Greatest Era" and "Undirectable Director"; two adaptations for the screen, *The Blue Hotel* and *The African Queen*; his novella, *The Morning Watch*; and finally his animal fable, "A Mother's Tale." The last years of his life were devoted almost entirely to film and television writing. In 1952 he wrote a five-part series for *Omnibus*, entitled "Mr. Lincoln." In 1953 he was at work on a film biography of Gauguin, *Noa Noa*. In 1954 he wrote a documentary story of the Tanglewood music festival. In 1955, at the time of his death, he had made preliminary sketches for a film for the Rockefeller project at Williamsburg, Virginia.

This study, begun as a doctoral dissertation, has been considerably revised since that time. It remains, however, a study of

Agee's development as an artist, and that treatment has dictated what has and has not been included for discussion. For instance, I have discussed those of Agee's poems which indicate development toward his best writing. The concerns which came into play here were that I do not consider the overall merit of Agee's poetry impressive, and because it has been well criticized, especially the collection in *Permit Me Voyage,* I did not feel an obligation to reread it in this study. The same criterion applies to the film writing. Although many of Agee's friends, David McDowell and Father Flye among them, believe Agee was, to quote McDowell, "working harder and better" toward the end of his life, I have argued in the final chapter that Agee's film work was a decline from his best conceptions. There are, as I have tried to indicate, a number of reasons—cultural, economic, psychological—for the decline. But what I am writing represents an unusual critical position. First, while I believe Agee was working harder in his last years, with even more discipline, I also believe that his film scripts amply demonstrate that he was not working any better. Second, there is a common belief that Agee was completing *A Death in the Family* toward the end of his life and that its quality offsets that of the film scripts. It is my conjecture, based on the evidence of his letters to Father Flye and on the themes found in the novel, especially in the manuscripts and notes, that Agee did very little work on his fictional autobiography after May 1950. For that reason the film scripts seem to me his final contribution. In discussing them I have nevertheless tried to keep my eye on the artist. I concentrate on those scripts to which I have had access to the notes and manuscripts, so that I can verify what Agee was creating. Again, there is more than enough criticism on Agee's work as a film adapter (for this reason I saw no harm, in fact good, in omitting discussion of *The Bride Comes to Yellow Sky* and *The Night of the Hunter*), but there is almost none on his artistry in film.

The same attention to aesthetic practice and theory has determined the focus of the remainder of this work. I repeat this point as a caution to readers of *Let Us Now Praise Famous Men* and of

Agee's film criticism. Much more can be said about both, especially the former. I might mention a comprehensive and, at times, brilliant discussion of *Famous Men* included in J. Douglas Perry's unpublished doctoral dissertation, and a very competent general discussion of the film criticism by Charles Mayo.[4] For this work I have chosen to emphasize the influence on *Famous Men* and Agee's film criticism of Stephen Dedalus' aesthetic in *A Portrait of the Artist as a Young Man* and of Joyce's concept of epiphany. Of course the whole question of aesthetics is a crucial one for modern literature, and in many ways Agee is the ideal figure to study for elucidating the problem. Torn between the romantic and modern movements, his life was a paradigm of Yeats's poem "The Choice"—to decide between perfecting his life or his art. As I have indicated in the first chapter of this study, Agee's religious background and continuing religious consciousness impressed upon him the need for a responsible morality toward others. Confronting this influence, however, was a need to express himself artistically. If his letters to Father Flye are typical, there was no time when Agee considered being anything other than a writer, unless it was a priest. And at the time, and specifically in Anglo-Catholicism, the two roles had a great deal in common. However, the role of the artist, especially as it was outlined by Keats and later by Joyce, was that of a passive spectator. The subject of the second chapter, then, is the accommodation Agee makes to this dilemma in his writing at Harvard.

Agee's earliest prose shows a competent imitation of naturalist and realist styles. Mainly he enjoyed satire and responded to the influence of Sinclair Lewis. His poetry, on the other hand, was more serious. First, it was more personal, more expressive of what he was feeling at the time. Second, it shows his keen appreciation of certain masters—Virgil, Whitman, Jeffers—yet his ability to use them for his own purposes. A hiatus in his poetic development— between 1928, when he wrote "Anne Garner," and 1930, when he wrote the "Epithalamium"—serves mainly as a transition between poetry and prose. The themes common to the three longer poems he had written while at Exeter I have called a corrupted mysticism, a belief that a union between God and man, or creator and creature, is destructive. Agee told Father Flye in the spring of 1929, these long poems expressed all he had to say "about nature and death." (*Letters,* p. 40). In his poetry at Harvard he therefore began to dedicate himself to learning his craft. He was aided in this endeavor by voracious reading of the English Metaphysical and Romantic poets and by the lectures of I. A. Richards. Richards made Agee aware of the full range of possibilities inherent in language, both psychological and creative. As well, he undoubtedly helped him to define, or led him to consider a definition of, the artistic process, for the subject preoccupies Agee's last two pieces of fiction written at Harvard. In these stories, "Death in the Desert" and "They That Sow in Sorrow Shall Reap," Agee was concerned with the application of certain restraints upon his feelings in order to discipline his expression. At the same time, however, he feared that discipline might affect his moral response toward others, and he was loath to make the application. The tentative resolution between art and life he achieved at Harvard was to make art a means to moral responsibility. Thus a definite pattern was beginning to emerge: he wanted, above all, to commit himself to some unvanquishable element, whether it was God or Truth or Art, and yet his continuing experience was consistent with the the themes of his early poetry—that a final union between matter and spirit is annihilation.

It must strike anyone as odd that such were Agee's utmost concerns in 1930. Because his mind was so committed to the eternal, he was wary of anything that smacked of the temporal. And the Great Depression was very temporal, as were the parties which sought to combat it. The one fact of his life at this time— which, if misunderstood, leads to a misreading of *Let Us Now Praise Famous Men*—is that Agee avoided all forms of partisanship. In the early 1940s he wrote a bitter autobiographical essay, later entitled "James Agee by Himself," in which he ridiculed his lack of political commitment. The following passage illustrates the point:

> *He was with Time Incorporated during the death of Calvin Coolidge. He was with the Loyalists heart and soul when André*

*Malraux spoke in the ballroom of the Hotel Roosevelt. He was with Borodin on a telescope when Shanghai fell on Rayna Prohme and Sheean got the wound that made him think. He was with Negley Farson on the follow-up. He was without funds at the time of the Nazi-Soviet pact. He found no peace. His suggestions as to the proper way first to avert the Second World War and, later, to end it, were universally rejected, but he bears no grudge toward any living creature. "Only wait," he likes to say. "Things will work themselves out in time." And thus far, none has dared to dispute it. [*Esquire *60 (December 1963):149]*

Thus, aside from his commercial writing for *Fortune* and a deeply personal and nihilistic film satire, "The House," Agee's work during the 1930s bore only a tangential relation to the contemporary scene. On the other hand, because he internalized all experience, his work bore a direct relation to the Depression and the various political and aesthetic questions which swept his friends in and out of the Communist party.

Nevertheless, it seems a more accurate reflection of Agee's work to concentrate in the third chapter on the poetic and prose experiments which led to the writing of *Let Us Now Praise Famous Men.* The fourth and fifth chapters, which concern *Famous Men* and his film criticism, logically follow this scheme. Throughout the 1930s Agee was developing a style he once called "Word Music." That is, he sought to use words as notes of music, stressing their aural effects. At the same time he saw a relation between words and images and, of course, the patterning of images in film. The result was to use language in much the same way as Joyce did in writing *Portrait* and *Ulysses,* as integers subject to and causative of innumerable modifications and significations. Furthermore, Agee expressed a sense of his Alabama experience that was tantamount to Joyce's definition of an epiphany, and the process by which he wrote the book closely resembles Dedalus' definition of an epic. Needless to say, *Famous Men* shows the profound influence of Joyce; and its aesthetic, because it equates the way in which music, image, and word can be used, serves as the basis for Agee's film criticism.

Oddly enough, the early 1940s are a creative vacuum in Agee's life. From the publication of *Famous Men* in 1941 until "Dedication Day" in 1946 there are only movie reviews, very few letters, and fewer anecdotes. Of course, "only" movie reviews is quite enough, for he wrote the kind of reviews which chronicle an era. As he watched more and more films, especially the documentaries and atrocity films of the war years, he became more impressed with the subjective nature of truth, with the particular biases by which data were selected, so that one truth and not another is revealed. The Atomic Bomb only increased his sense that the nation was asleep and that he, if no one else, must wake himself before consciousness was obliterated. This feeling in essence is what prompted him to leave *Time* to finish the autobiographical novel, *A Death in the Family*, which he had begun in 1947. Though he never completed it, the impulse to renew his own values is important and is recorded throughout unpublished poems, rough drafts of essays, and discarded sections of the novel. The sixth chapter traces this creative reaction from its formation to its ultimate statement in "A Mother's Tale."

Unfortunately, what I take to be a significant part of Agee's reaction to the Bomb, postwar humanism, and liberalism, contained in a number of letters Agee wrote to Whittaker Chambers, is missing from the record. They were reportedly destroyed in a fire at Chambers's Maryland farm. Chambers writes glowingly about Agee in his two books, *Witness* and *Cold Friday*, but has very little to say about their relationship. The only vestiges of Agee's reaction to Chambers' investigation and the Hiss trials is a comment to Father Flye—to the effect that he was following Jim Ball's dispatches to *Time*—and a rough draft of a letter, perhaps never sent, to John Crowe Ransom, declining an invitation to review *Witness* because "the whole business involves me so on the 'creative' level, that I must doubt my rightness, as well as ability, in trying to approach it critically." [5]

The last chapter, as mentioned, concerns Agee's declining sensibility. As a screen writer he mainly worked at adapting another writer's conception to a new medium. On the whole he did a good, and at times an extraordinary, job. But it is his "original" material that betrays him. Agee's increasing reliance upon subjective camera techniques to reveal conceptions he had already brought to life in literature is reason enough to suspect a decline in his work. His self-indulgent conception of the artist in *Noa Noa* and *Tanglewood Story* reveals the real distintegration taking place within him. I do not personally enjoy the unhappy ending of this study, but it is not inconsistent. Agee's final failures actually reveal the intense contradictions which gave birth to great art. Even though I have taken the title of this last chapter, "The Full Life is Full of Crap," from a letter Agee wrote to Father Flye, I suspect that it indicates my own disposition much more than Agee's. It seems to me he would not have had it any other way.

Acknowledgments I would like the reader to know that without the help of the following people, there would be no book. For that reason I am truly grateful.

First of all, to Jules Chametzky, who helped me in every way to see my own thoughts, and to Victor Kramer, Fred Turner, and Seymour Rudin.

Secondly, to David McDowell, Father James Harold Flye, Dwight Macdonald, and Howard Taubman.

Thirdly, to the staff of the manuscript collection at the University of Texas Library, Mrs. Mary Hirth and Mrs. Lois Bell Garcia and Mr. John Payne, to Martin Hubbard, Reference Librarian of the University of Massachusetts, to Professor Edward C. Moore, former Dean of the Graduate School of the University of Massachusetts, and to the library staff of the St. Helena Public Library, Betty Reed and Joyce Scharf.

And for long suffering and joy, to Marg.

St. Helena, California, 1971

James Rufus Agee was born on November 27, 1909, in Knoxville, Tennessee. His father, Hugh James Agee—or "Jay," as he was called—was a native Tennessean, raised on the Cumberland Plateau near La Follete, some twenty-five miles northwest of Knoxville. The family traced its decent through farmers and doctors to Mathieu Agee, a Frenchman who sided with William of Orange in 1688 and received a Virginia land grant in consideration. At the time of Rufus' birth, Jay was employed by his father-in-law, Joel Tyler, who owned a lumber business in Knoxville. The marriage of Laura Tyler and Jay Agee had not been looked upon favorably by the Tylers. Laura was a University of Tennessee graduate, the daughter of the first woman to receive a master's degree from the University of Michigan. Her sister Paula was a pianist, her brother Hugh a painter, not to slight her older sister Jessie, who founded an order of nuns in the Episcopal Church. Agee, on the other hand, despite experience as a teacher, had only a fourth-grade education; when they met in 1904, he was working for the Post Office Department. Laura Tyler's attraction to him was unshakable, however, and deep enough to prod her to take her brother Hugh to Panama, where Agee had been transferred and where she married him in the summer of 1906. There is more than a little significance to this romance—suggesting as it does Laura Tyler's individuality and rebelliousness as well as the magnetic quality of Jay Agee's kindness and gentleness. These were the traits they passed on to their firstborn, Rufus.

The Agees remained in Panama for two years. When they returned, it was to Jay's home in La Follette, where he worked for a short time for the Louisville and Nashville Railroad before taking the position with his father-in-law in Knoxville. When Rufus was born, the family was living at 1505 Highland Avenue, a short walk from his maternal grandparents, who lived on Clinch Street.

Knoxville at the time has been described by Joseph Wood Krutch as "thoroughly provincial";[1] certainly nothing James Agee was to write about it would ever contradict that estimate. In an atmosphere of Southern family closeness prior to the First World War—the "contemporaneous atmosphere" Agee recreates so vividly in "Knoxville: Summer of 1915"—Rufus grew up. He has written so well of his childhood in *A Death in the Family* that nothing need be added. His family friends remember him as precocious and quick and polite, not unlike the fictional Rufus. However, they also remember that the real Rufus preferred classical myths and medieval legends to the usual children's fairy tales.

Following his father's untimely death in 1916 (the central incident in *A Death in the Family*), Rufus began public school. He also studied painting with his Uncle Hugh and music with his Aunt Paula. In the summer of 1919 his mother rented a cottage for the season on the grounds of St. Andrew's School in Monteagle, Tennessee. Located at the southern end of the Cumberland Plateau, St. Andrew's was operated specifically for boys of mountain parents by a monastic order of the Episcopal Church, the Fathers of the Holy Cross. It is more than likely that it was to provide the boy with masculine guidance as well as religious instruction that, when the opportunity to rent the cottage extended past the summer, Mrs. Agee decided to stay on and to enter Rufus in St. Andrew's. "Thus came about," as his oldest friend and confidant, Father James Harold Flye, writes in introduction to his collection of Agee's letters, "the friendship to which this book bears witness" (*Letters*, p. 12).

It is important to note this friendship, as well as other elements of Agee's life at St. Andrew's, for their significance to his later life and writing cannot be overlooked. Although the fact is not included in his characterization of Richard in *The Morning Watch*, Agee was an extraordinary student for St. Andrew's. According to his former classmates, his background in literature and art put him well ahead of the typical mountain boys attending the school. What ought to be noted in this connection is that Agee never thought of himself as extraordinary. The shyness was natural, though complicated, and perhaps its source can be glimpsed in the first chapter of *A Death in the Family*, when Rufus puzzles over his father's admonition not to brag. Bragging, Rufus mistakenly concludes, has to do with fighting, with bravery and courage. "Don't you brag you're smart if you're not brave," he reminds himself. "You've got nothing to brag about" (p. 21).

Agee represents his own shyness here as a sense of failure to live up to what he presumes his father expects. It is not difficult, then, to imagine the effect upon him of a religious tradition that asks man to live up to God's expectations. The difficulty lies in detecting the sources of its ambiance: a magnificent antiauthoritarianism dwelling in what both Father Flye and Robert Fitzgerald have accurately termed an *anima naturaliter Christiana*.[2] While Father Flye describes the religious atmosphere at St. Andrew's as "strong and persuasive, but of a friendly, natural unaffected quality" (*Letters,* p. 11), the conflict Agee depicts in *The Morning Watch* is the attempt to relate religious images and discipline to an awakening intellectual and emotional identity. Of course the school only reinforced the piety which had surrounded Rufus throughout his childhood. His mother was very devout, and this trait in her irked him, as can be inferred from his characterization of Mary in *A Death in the Family*. His Aunt Jessie—prototype for Aunt Hannah in the novel and founder of a religious sisterhood affiliated with the Order of the Holy Cross—was, according to Father Flye, imbued with the idea of a "great stream of continuity" which included the Roman Catholic, Anglo-Catholic, and Orthodox Churches. To some extent Agee continued to give allegiance to the formal Anglican tradition—he was baptized and buried in it and gave testimony to it in his 1934 prose poem, "Dedication"—but perhaps most essential to his continuing religious consciousness, especially after his lapse from formal communion, was his long friendship with Father Flye.

Father Flye has written that the friendship was "a happy, frank and sincere one of affection and respect on both sides, with the realization of a bond of understanding and the sharing in many basic feelings, instincts and sympathies such as can give the sense of real companionship in spirit" (*Letters,* p. 12). But that may only have been the nub of it. The friendship began out of ordinary human needs—the Flyes were childless and Agee fatherless—and lasted a lifetime. Father Flye was not only a surrogate father, then, but also a priest, a spiritual father. Moreover, Mrs. Flye was a sensitive and creative person, a painter, with whom Agee always felt a deep affinity, and her husband was, and is, a literate and compassionate human being. These are the incalculable elements which form the rich texture of this relationship and of which a reader must constantly remind himself. For ultimately, it might be argued, the friendship Agee shared with Father Flye served him as a standard of what love of man and love of God could be. Certainly more than any other experience, more than his formal religious training, it was the consistent influence of this friendship, coupled with a haunting love for the people and places of the Cumberland Plateau, which Agee carried away with him from St. Andrew's School.

At the conclusion of the primary grades in 1924, Rufus with his mother and sister Emma moved back to Knoxville. They lived for a short time with his grandparents, the Tylers, before Mrs. Agee married Erskine Wright, a priest she had met at St. Andrew's. After a brief stay in South Carolina the Wrights made a permanent move to Rockland, Maine. Rufus stayed on in Knoxville to complete the school year, at the end of which he bicycled for a few weeks through England and France with Father Flye. When he returned to America, it was to enter Phillips Academy in Exeter, New Hampshire, where most readers meet him. His first published letter to Father Flye is dated October 1925—that is, during his first month at the school. His most ambitious early poem, "Anne Garner," was written in the spring of his senior year. In the two-and-a-half-year interim he published a total of twelve poems, both lyric and narrative, sixteen pieces of fiction, three plays, and assorted essays and reviews in the *Phillips Exeter Monthly.* Most of these pieces are marked by precociousness as well as uncertainty, but they present a bewildering, and sometimes revealing, array of starts and experiments. For instance, two early stories, "The Bell Tower of Amiens" and "The Scar," as well as the short poem "Beauvais," are typically Gothic, but they are not set in time-worn but in war-gutted churches of post-First World War Europe.[3] Some satiric pieces, such as "Jenkinsville" and "Knoxton High," show the influence of Sinclair Lewis, John Dos Passos, and Sherwood Anderson and suggest some of the spirit but none of the gall nor audacity of Agee's later work. However, a light touch was distinctive of the period. Not only did he deplore Lewis' "bitterness" in a review of *Elmer Gantry*, he was also looking for "finesse" and "rapier-like delicacy" in satire. Moreover, he was at an age when he could toy with the idea of a "Memorial" High School, its doughboy statue on the front lawn inscribed "IT WAS HELL, BUDDY," or write such delightful paragraphs as

Jenkinsville has a White Way. It is a hundred yards long, and it leads from the depot straight to the Court House. It is lighted at regular intervals by very new, very chaste, street lamps, and it has been carelessly splashed with asphalt, which lies along the street's centre like a tattered and wrinkled ribbon. At the Court House, however, all improvements end in a dusty loop, well shaded, and frequented by mountaineers, hounds, sows, and other animals.[4]

The fact of the matter is that Rufus Agee was a seventeen-year-old American, New England preppie, writing about a past which had not yet fully touched him. His letters are full of "swell" talk about courses and grades, books, movies, music, and people, but the first and only hint of an emotional experience occurs at the beginning of his senior year (in November 1927) when he tells Father Flye he had "had a perfectly frightful spring" (*Letters,* p. 31). In an earlier letter, dated June 16, 1927, and addressed to Exeter alumnus, Dwight Macdonald, Agee had explained that the trauma concerned the breakup of a friendship similar to one Macdonald had written of in fiction. "In my case," Agee wrote, "there were consequences which you may possibly have thought of but did not suggest—I was almost drowned in psychological meandering too dreary and far too long for any story. Quite frequently I've been on the verge of suicide." Whatever the details of this affair, it is significant that he did not feel impelled to write about it. One reason can be derived from another letter to Father Flye, written only months before the breakup. Concerning the news of a friend's suicide, Agee told Flye:

It brings me a little nearer realizing the difference between such a thing in fact and fiction. As I am now, I am able to read and write of the most sordid sad things with rather impersonal interest; but as I come into actual contact with more and more gore, I have a more ghastly experience as a background for my literature.... I realize that before long I shall be quite as disgusted and horrified by realism as, say, Mother. [Letters, p. 25]

It is clear from this excerpt that acquiring experience was no way for Rufus Agee to create fiction. His underlying fear here, which remained with him throughout his life, was that his response to experience was simply unmanageable. In his own words, it was "far too long for any story," and his reaction was to keep his life and his art as separate as possible.

The comment does explain, however, the surface calm of his writing at Exeter. Although at times there are jarring inconsistencies, brought about mainly by an attempt to fit Tennessee mountain dialect into Grecian myth and medieval legend, there is an acceptance of a narrative point of view. Only once, in "Between Trains," does Agee attempt to switch or mix points of view as he later did in *A Death in the Family*. Using a transitional device from cinema, moving to a new point of view as a previous one leaves the scene, Agee places the unsettled, lonely interior monologue of a drifter in contrast to the self-assertive, brash talk of a traveling salesman. "Between Trains" and other Exeter stories—"Sentimental Journey," "Bound for the Promised Land," even "Chivalry An Allegory"—show the distinct influence of Hemingway.[5] Derivative or not, the perspective of the opening sentence of "Between Trains" ("The little golden squares of the departing train were shuttered by the thickening trees") is reminiscent of "The Battler" ("Nick stood up. He was all right. He looked up the track at the lights of the caboose going out of sight around a curve.") [6] His themes are also similar to those of Hemingway, Fitzgerald, and Anderson: loneliness, a lack of emotional fulfillment each of which pertains in the Exeter stories to the broader theme of illusion and reality.

The most complex, though surely not the best, treatment of this theme is found in "Chivalry An Allegory," the story of a young knight who takes chivalry for granted. Edwin leaves his mother and peasant girlfriend for the court of the king. On the way he must rescue a fair damsel and her father from distress. By doing so, he wins her hand and her father's land. But after many years he finds out that his moment of combat had been a sham staged by his wife's father. Disillusioned, the young knight decides to return to his boyhood home. But he finds that his mother is dead, his former girlfriend married, and his family castle in the hands of a tyrant. His girl, however, pleads with him to save her family and friends from slavery. But Edwin's challenge goes unanswered. Whether he had learned his lesson or only that a bird in the hand is worth two in the bush, Edwin returns to his wife, suggesting a second honeymoon. Certainly Agee's treatment is overdone. Having the characters speak a variety of Tennessee dialects only makes them more oafish than they ought to be as well as dispelling any poignancy the story might have had. Nevertheless, the theme of hopeful ideals undercut by experience is directly communicated, and its later successful treatment in "A Mother's Tale" is brought to mind.

The complexity of "Chivalry An Allegory" is the result of its plot. Most of the stories Agee wrote at Exeter were simply character sketches, from the naturalism of "Minerva Farmer" to the surrealism of "Sacre Du Printemps." [7] It is therefore not difficult to understand how, or even why, he could write as he had told Father Flye "the most sordid sad things with rather impersonal interest" (*Letters,* p. 25). Obviously the disillusionment of his characters, their failure to realize themselves or the events which overcome them, were feelings he shared with the naturalists and realists he was reading. They do not, however, seem the result of any deeply felt experience, certainly not in the way some of his poems are. Although most of his lyrics are simply mood pieces, two of them, "Ebb Tide" and "Widow," grow out of brooding over the death of his father. And his longer poems—"Menalcas," "Pygmalion," and "Anne Garner"—which express themes typical in adolescent poetry—sex, creativity, nature—are at the very least ambitious and precocious expressions of emotions he actually felt. The point is basic: even though Agee was to confess to Father Flye a few months after he had finished "Anne Garner" that he could not write "lyrics—*subjective* things" (*Letters*, p. 38), the fact remains that he and others considered these poems his best work. It was "Menalcas" which his good friend, W. M. "Brick" Frohock passed on to S. Foster Damon in the spring of 1928 and "Menalcas" and "Pygmalion" which Agee later showed to Robert Frost. "The general verdict," Agee wrote Flye, "is that I can do a lot if I don't give up" (*Letters*, p. 37). The effect of this professional encouragement was understandably exhilarating. He would not have to conform to what in 1928 might be expected from an Exeter-Harvard education, to sell stocks and bonds, nor to the popular image of the struggling American writer who wrote ad copy. James R. Agee was a poet and, for the moment at least, convinced enough of his talent to declare, "I'll croak before I write ads or sell bonds" (*Letters*, p. 37).

Essential to the composition of these three long poems was Agee's reading of Walt Whitman. "I've been feeling something," he wrote to Father Flye in December 1927,

—a sort of universal—oh, I don't know, feeling the beauty of everything, not excluding slop-jars and foetuses—and a feeling of love for everything—and now I've run into Walt Whitman. [Letters, p. 34]

Most of Agee's critics have overestimated the importance of these lines, for the Whitman influence, though seminal, seems to have been short-lived.[8] Little more than a year and a half later, on May 10, 1929, in response to Dwight Macdonald's criticism of "Anne Garner," Agee wrote to him:

I went through the W. Whitman stage about a year ago; and he

seems generally half-assed to me now, wherever I open the book.
My first reaction to your criticism was: "Yes,—but at the time it
was the best thing that could possibly happen to American writ-
ing. Where would, say, Jeffers, be without him?" Now I'm not so
sure that if Jeffers had lived at that time, he wouldn't have writ-
ten much the same things he does now. I don't believe Walt had a
hell of a lot of influence: but I still enjoy the idea of such stuff
appearing when it did. I think if you boiled some of his stuff
down and expressed it decently you'd get a few damned fine
pictures and poetry: he was sometimes more than an ecstatic
young gent flexing his thighs and letting the wind tear up his hair.

These remarks seem to indicate that at one point Agee was willing
to accept Whitman's influence but upon examination became
anxious to reject it. For instance, there is a revealing defen-
siveness in his statement, "I don't believe Walt had a hell of a lot
of influence." After all, how could Agee deny the influence in
these lines from his "Pygmalion"?

I press my face into the hot, sweet earth,
And hear the steady singing of the sap,
And feel the prickling grass against my cheek—
Trees! Thy red buds unfolding stickily—[9]

There is the free verse, the repeated coordinate phrasing, and the
sensuous descriptions found in the poetry of Whitman. However,
grant the barbaric yawp (ascribable to "feeling the beauty of
everything"), and differences emerge which indicate the limits of
the Whitman influence.

Despite the evidence of this verse, it is clear that when Agee
wrote to Macdonald, he did not admire Whitman as a versifier.
Furthermore, these remarks are substantially repeated in Agee's
1942 review of Hugh d'Anson Fausset's biography of Whitman. [10]
What appealed to him was Whitman's mysticism, the apprehension of unity in diversity, expressed in transcendentalism by the
concept of the Oversoul. This same tendency was at the basis of
Agee's sensibility. It is important, however, to note the distinctions
Agee began to express even in these early poems, for in his

later work they resulted in a magnificent and unresolved tension between the cosmic and the mundane. "Pygmalion," for instance, is written from the point of view of God, but the poem recounts God's incommunicable love for His creation. Like Lennie in Steinbeck's *Of Mice and Men,* Agee's God cannot touch His beloved without crushing her. The poem ends as almost a surprise for the poet, with God clasping the world to His breast and thus destroying it. Variations of this corrupted mysticism are also found in "Menalcas." Written in vague imitation of a Greek tragedy, "Menalcas" shows the influence of Robinson Jeffers in Agee's borrowing, "This black uncomprehending skull of stone," from "Roan Stallion" [11] —"The small dark head under his nostrils: a small round stone, that smelt human, black hair growing from it" (l. 238). It was therefore no accident that Agee spoke of Whitman and Jeffers in the same paragraph of his May 1929 letter to Macdonald. However, he did not seem to be aware then of what has become a critical commonplace:

Jeffers seems a good deal like Whitman at times—and, of course, a good deal more besides. I don't at all mean he takes a good dose of Walt before he works; he may never have heard of him, for all I know—but in the way he says things. I have the same feeling that his hands are too big for the keys.

Agee was no more interested in Jeffers style than he was in Whitman's. What chiefly interested him was the subject that interested a good many American poets in the 1920s and 1930s, from Hart Crane to Ezra Pound—an attempt to find a modern historical synthesis by recreating ancient myth and folk legend in contemporary poetic language. "Menalcas," a closet verse drama, concerns a king who has doomed his kingdom by an incestuous marriage to his daughter. To expiate the curse, the Chorus suggests that Menalcas kill the demented son of the marriage, a suggestion he quickly accepts before he kills himself to end the play. There is little in the blank verse to recommend it. However, the failure of love through pride places "Menalcas" in important juxtaposition to the themes of "Pygmalion" and "Anne Garner."

Looking back on the composition of "Anne Garner" [12] after its publication in *Permit Me Voyage*, Agee noted:

This I did after running a second-string mile in the rain in 1928 had brought me to bed for a free week with tonsilitis. It's that kind of poem. I was eighteen and ill-read (though I bluffed a lot) and I meant every word of it. [13]

What he "meant every word of" can best be seen by comparing the poem to its obvious predecessor, Jeffers' "Roan Stallion." [14] The attempt to weave myth and natural symbols into a setting of the Tennessee mountains of course parallels Jeffers' work. Agee's story, however, contains significant variations. Jeffers' poem concerns a woman, abused in her marriage, who in her simple, religious way perceives in a stallion a likeness to the power which effected the Incarnation. California is drawn to mate with the stallion. Revolted, then, by her husband's advances, she seeks the stallion's protection. The horse kills the man, and California, "moved by some obscure human fidelity" (ll. 300) kills the horse. Like California, Anne Garner is an earth-mother symbol; like her, also, she does not find her marriage fulfilling. "Anne Garner," however, opens with childbirth, a scene Agee uses later to portray the birth of Lincoln in his television scripts for *Omnibus*. The fruit of Anne's marriage is stillborn. She buries the child as the poet sings:

Let the blood of the babe to the hidden wells
Of life drain downward.
Let him live in womb and womb of earth,
In the swelling seed of every plant
Let him live.

[ll. 54-59]

Thus, while Anne spins out the thread of her life, she sees the changes of season and natural growth and harvest as the result of her buried flesh. The poet tells us that she becomes a farmer's talisman and begins to "look upon herself as earth" (l. 302). She cannot die "save in some great/Catastrophe of all the universe" (ll. 325-26). And after such an event takes place, her dead body is found by her husband on top of the burial plot of her stillborn child.

It is about the circumstances of her death, however, that Agee's Exeter version, most probably written in late April or early May 1928, comes into significant conflict with his revision of the poem, published in the spring 1929 issue of *Hound and Horn* and unaltered for *Permit Me Voyage*. Describing Anne's relation to the universe, the Exeter version reads:

> *She rose, and from the height of naked pasture*
> *Watched the stars slowly swing across the sky,*
> *Or brooded above the dark, wide fields that flowed*
> *Into the starlight, cradling the life*
> *That surged up through the earth.*
> *All, all was life,—*
> *High in the sky the stars pulsed rhythmically,*
> *And in the earth, the seeds surged toward the light,*
> *And mists rose from the fields and from still water,*
> *Bearing that life out to infinity.*
>
> *[ll. 280-88]*

The same passage in revision reads:

> *She rose, and from the height of naked pasture*
> *Watched the stars slowly swing across the sky,*
> *Or brooded above the dark, wide fields that flowed*
> *Into the starlight, cradling the life*
> *That blindly moved within.*
> *Life was in death:*
> *The world rolled black and barren in its mists,*
> *And life was locked deep in the sheathing snows.*
>
> *[PMV, p. 31, ll. 251-58]*

The reasons for this revision can be explained with the help of two more comparisions. In the revised version the "great Catastrophe of all the universe" is the "fearsome falling of the stars,/ The blasting of evil and the doom of earth" (ll. 304-05), whereas in the original, Agee had been more explicit: "the world's end, the Second Coming of Christ" (l. 347). What takes place during that catastrophe, however, is not clearly portrayed in either version. In the original, the "greater sower,"

> . . . *sows the universe anew,*
> *Advancing toward this pasture-land,*
> *Whereon she stands. Advancing, sowing.*
> *Bringer of life of the newer sowing.*

[*ll. 384–87*]

Yet in this instance it is in the revision that the poet is more explicit:

> *He sows the universe anew,*
> *Advancing toward her pasture-land,*
> *Arms flexed above her, blotting the sky*
> *With body bent to the world's rim.*

[*ll. 343–46*]

Agee's intention can be gleaned perhaps only by comparing the two versions. Either consciously or unconsciously, he obscures the point in both. The story Agee wanted to tell is apparently that of a world, or "earth" as symbolized by Anne, yearning for the touch of Christ. Once received, that touch ends mortal life and brings eternal satisfaction. Agee tries to make this point in the revision by specifying a distinction between the life force in the heavens, which is eternal life, and the life force of earth Anne has come to represent, which is material and hence subject to death. Thus he changes the mystical "All, all was life" to the more orthodox "Life was in death." On the other hand, the revision lacks the audacity—if that is the proper term—to suggest Anne's copulation with Christ. One interpretation is that Agee tried to make the conclusion of his revision more "natural." He speaks of "the doom of earth," not "the world's end, the Second Coming of Christ." As well, his "greater sower" in the revision could be merely some heavenly life force, not the Alpha and Omega of apocalyptic tradition. In this respect Agee may have realized that Jeffers was dealing with a safer metaphor. California's motives, though ostensibly Christian, are based on pagan myth—copulation with the gods in the form of animals. Agee specifically avoids such a meaning in both versions of his poem. Anne confronts a bull in her barn but makes no mythic connection such as California's. However, in denying her this plausible desire, Agee has committed her to participation in the fantastic— not merely the end of the world and the Second Coming of Christ but, if we are to take seriously "the chisellings of lust" Anne's husband notices on her dead face, copulation with the Son of God. Because Agee's revision is without precedent in Christian revelation, as well as without the transcendental mysticism of his Exeter version, it is more than likely that he felt the union should be merely suggested.

It is necessary to underline these revisions in light of "Pygmalion" and "Menalcas." In each of these poems Agee is describing the relationship between God and His creation and, on another level, the relationship between the artist and his art. In each instance there is an inability of the Creator to properly love His creation, to see it for what it is and to respect its essential otherness. God crushes the world in an excess of adoration. Menalcas mates with his daughter and kills the progeny as well as himself. Anne and the life force she has come to represent are destroyed by a union with the eternal. The variations on this theme, as well as the progress of revisions in "Anne Garner," indicate not only Agee's externalization of his personal, creative dilemma—his attempt to objectify himself from the objects of his consciousness—but also suggest the very sure sense of evil—"original sin" in the words of his Anglo-Catholic catechism—that resided at the heart of his essentially mystic sensibility.

It is important to note here that these aspects of Agee's "romanticism" had roots in times and places other than nineteenth-century America. The animism and violent natural imagery which pervade these poems, especially "Anne Garner," can be traced to Virgil's *Aeneid* more surely than to Whitman's *Leaves of Grass*. Similarly, the mystical tendency of the poet was more probably rooted in the seventeenth-century Catholic meditative tradition than in the "inner light" of American Quakerism or the Great Awakening. These distinctions are important, for they suggest the undeniably broad ground upon which Agee was to erect a literary mansion. It was no accident that he shared the disillusionment of the expatriates, for he shared in a process of deracination similar to that held by Malcolm Cowley to have been so influential on the lost generation. Agee had lost his father at the age of six. He had left his home ground at fifteen. He had been reared in a religious tradition with deeper roots in medieval and reformation Europe than in eighteenth- or nineteenth-century America. In many respects he was better prepared to become a great writer than was the generation before him, except that he had not-learned or experienced the advantage of looking back. He had left the South just when the effects of the First World War were forcing Southern writers to reclaim their heritage. He had begun to live in New England at the tail end of an economic boom he had little means of understanding or of assessing. What is more, and perhaps most important, he had no way of getting away to look back. His struggle to escape romantic antinomies, the effort to distinguish between the self and the objects of perception and memory, was not be gained at Cowley's French Line pier but only, as Walker Evans has pointed out, at great personal cost.

"One of the heaviest problems and contradictions within me," James Agee wrote, probably no later than 1935, "is that of the human being vs the artist." And he added a particularly individual touch: "Which resolves itself, ultimately, into the Battle of the Centuries: God vs Art" ("Reflections on *PMV*"). As he indicated, the question of life and art was hardly unique to himself. At least in its relation to the twentieth century, it had its beginnings in the efforts of the Romantic poets to break the stranglehold of Cartesian epistemology: that the only valid reality was the thinking self. Their approach was to verify objective reality by their emotional responses and inner feelings. (Dr. Johnson's pain from kicking the stone was the beginning—or the end if you will—of the Romantic era). Inevitably this method led to the primacy of subjectivity and the search for new forms of expression—for feelings had shapes that could be represented only by freer, newer forms. The particularly American approach to the question is influenced by the Lockean tradition, which is dependent on and responsive to the significance of sense knowledge. It is already evident in the early writings of Jonathan Edwards and continues through the prose of Emerson and Thoreau to the naturalists and realists of the late nineteenth and twentieth centuries. This approach emphasizes the "fact" or the "experience" more than the observer or the participant, because they are believed to be symbolic of a greater, hidden reality. Yet because of the central role of the artist either as respondent or as reporter, both traditions contain the danger of egotistical excess: the writer becomes priest or prophet of a new religion of art, separate from the common, material, and technological concerns of "life."

In a way bound to form strange contradictions, James Agee inherited elements from both traditions. For instance, when he was writing Dwight Macdonald about movies on July 21, 1927—

Chapter 2
A Portrait
of the Artist
as a Young
Man

the summer before his Exeter senior year—that he did not see "how much more can be done with writing or with the stage," that "in fact, every kind of recognized 'art' has been worked pretty nearly to the limit," he was commenting on the possibility of artistic forms available to his experience. And when he later confessed to Father Flye that the most difficult aspect of his ambition was "to decide what I want to write and in exactly what way" (*Letters,* p. 46), he was describing a common Romantic dilemma—that of a plethora of feelings which were confusing rather than concentrated in any one particular shape. Such a situation, incidentally, points to the essentially passive role the Romantic artist assumes in the face of experience; that is, he must wait until reality affects him in such a way that his response is as intelligible as it is spontaneous. It is not unusual, therefore, to encounter artistic strategies such as are found in Agee's letters; they are no different in this respect from the notebooks of Coleridge, Wordsworth's "Preface," or the letters of Keats.

Keats, in fact, offers an instructive parallel. When shortly before his twenty-first birthday Agee wrote Father Flye that he had to make his "mind as broad and deep and rich as possible, as quick and fluent as possible; abnormally sympathetic and yet perfectly balanced" (*Letters,* p. 47), Keats's "vale of Soul-making" and "Negative Capability" spring to mind. [1] With these phrases Keats had defined the purpose of his life, to acquire a soul or identity, and the proper strategy of the artist, to be capable of "being in uncertainties." It might seem that life and art were opposites for Keats—"Soul-making" a moral effort, the definition of character by choice; "Negative Capability," a choiceless, amoral perspective. It is necessary to note, however, that Keats spoke of "Soul-making" as a passive encounter with reality—"How then are Souls to be made?" And perhaps more to the point: "the heart must feel and suffer in a thousand diverse ways!" In these phrases "Soul-making" is a component of "Negative Capability" or, to use Agee's terms, it is an effort to be "abnormally sympathetic" to all aspects of reality in order to create a "perfectly balanced" sensibility. Ideally, then,

28
A Portrait
of the Artist
as a Young
Man

art and life are compatible in Keats' aesthetic. The contradictions arising in Agee's case are implied precisely in his restatement of the dilemma: "the human being vs the artist" or "God vs Art." In other words, Agee sees his life as having moral ramifications other than those which would perfect his sensibility as an artist. When Agee wrote Father Flye of his decision to be a writer, he concluded that:

29
A Portrait
of the Artist
as a Young
Man

> *The whole thing still seems just within the bounds of possible achievement; but highly improbable. There are too many other things crowding in to ruin it: the whole course of everyday life. And yet, of course, it's absolutely necessary for me to live as easily and calmly and fully as I can; and to be and feel human rather than coldblooded about the whole thing. It's only too easy, I find, to be "Human." I care as much as I ever did about other people's feelings, and worry much more when I hurt them. Of course I should be and am thankful for this, but it certainly helps complicate matters. [Letters, p. 49]*

Here is the essential difference between fact and fiction and, quite possibly, the difference between the English Keats and the American Agee. "Facts" or "experience" have a moral significance which demands that they be respected for what they are rather than for what they can be to art. Art, on the other hand, demands cold-bloodedness. That prescription is the core of Agee's dilemma that life and art are at odds. It is also the goad to his intense struggle to make them the same.

Nowhere does this struggle emerge with more urgency than in Agee's writing between 1930 and 1940. For during this chaotic decade he came of age: not merely by passing his twenty-first birthday, graduating from college, securing his first job; but also by formulating his intention to be a writer and by the events that led up to and proceeded from that decision. The lines from the letter quoted above were written in November 1930, when Agee was starting his junior year at Harvard. As he explained in this letter and in a later one, he had abandoned plans to quit school— first, to bum to California for a job in the movies; next, to seek a

30
A Portrait
of the Artist
as a Young
Man

teaching position. He had also given up ambitions to direct films or to compose music. The spring of 1930 had been decisive for him. Until then he had published only a few poems in the *Harvard Advocate*. Written in the metaphysical manner, they recapitulated his themes from "Menalcas," "Pygmalion," and "Anne Garner"—mortality, the paradox of love and death, and the medieval theme of *carpe diem*. However, Agee saw very little significance either personal or poetic to these poems. As he wrote to Macdonald in 1929 concerning "The Rendezvous": "a malformed bastard of Donne and Hardy." He explained his slowed output to Father Flye as a reaction to "Anne Garner." That poem, he noted, had expressed everything he had wanted "to say or feel about nature and death. . . . So," he continued, "ever since, when I've really wanted to write—I've been unable to, because anything I could think of seemed so far below that in standard and opportunity" (*Letters*, p. 40). However, by January 1930 he was at work on a new, long poem, which he finished toward the beginning of April. In a letter to Macdonald of January 17, 1930, he called it "a sort of inverted Epithalamium," presumably because it progresses from night to day rather than from day to night as in Spenser's poem. Later reflecting on its publication in *Permit Me Voyage*, he was to write: "You read poetry at Harvard and that's what you get. Derivative to the rectum" ("Reflections on *PMV*"). At the same time, however, he noted that it had a "fair subtlety and durability of Word Music"—a phrase which places it distinctly in Agee's progress to maturity as an artist.[2]

"Word Music" describes an ideal Agee worked to achieve in poetry throughout the early 1930s. Like most writers of the period, he was preoccupied with creating a unique poetic diction. But this effort was not merely a reflection of revivified nationalism kept afloat by the postwar boom; it was an aesthetic necessity for him as a Romantic artist. The closest analogy with his inner feelings and response to reality was in music; hence it was the effect he sought when expressing his response in words. In "Epithalamium" he began by experimenting with recurrent phrasing—actually musical restatements in the manner of Renaissance verse forms, such as the rondel and the sestina. Similarly, he extended the animated natural imagery of "Anne Garner," which contrasts the movements of the heavens and the earth, to provide a frame for his wedding hymn. His preference for this diurnal metaphor goes back to his Exeter poem, "Orbs Terrae" and his reading of the *Aeneid*. He was later to fuse these two lines of development—musical form and animated nature—in a never completed poem begun in 1933, "Theme and Variations."

31
A Portrait
of the Artist
as a Young
Man

Although Agee had pointed out to Father Flye in his letter of November that the medium to achieve his goal would be the narrative poetry of "Epithalamium"—"prose," he argued, "holds you down from the possibility of such music" (*Letters*, p. 48)—he had used similar musical devices in a short story, "Death in the Desert," published in the *Harvard Advocate* in October 1930 (117:16–24). The story contains at least two instances of recurrent phrasing. Agee ends the story with a phrase of advice he hears at the beginning. This kind of summation—a narrator recalling what he has heard as a character—is not uncommon. The second instance—repetition within the same point of view—is more significant, especially in light of his use of the device in poetry.

"Death in the Desert" concerns a young hitchhiker who is picked up by an Oklahoma couple. Forced to listen to the couple's trivial conversation, and in pain from a boil on his ear, he retreats into an interior monologue in which he guesses at the couple's susceptibility for advertising ("The man at the filling station is trained to help you" [*Prose*, p. 76]), imagines the couple as skeletons, mixing that image with that of a girl they stop to help ("a confusion of lovely flesh and Oklahoma bones wasn't as amusing as you might think" [*Prose*, p. 77]), then plunges into a memory of Tennessee woods in an effort to recall a feeling of former tranquility ("I tried now, knew I would fail, and failed, to feel about it as I had when I was eleven "[*Prose*, p. 78]). Agee characterizes this monologue as a "state that passed for sleep, most of the time, now that I was bumming" (*Prose*, p. 75); and it is this phrase which recurs at the end of the story, after the car has hit a bump, jolting the narrator to consciousness

32
A Portrait
of the Artist
as a Young
Man

to witness the driver mercilessly bypassing a delirious Negro stumbling in the middle of the road. Following the incident, the narrator's moral introspection is counterpointed by the couple's accusations of one another. The narrator concludes that he is going to let "well enough alone," that at least for a while he had "thought clearly and well: so clearly and so well that thought assumed substance and shape," but that finally, ironically, it was a "state that passed for sleep now that I was bumming" (*Prose*, p. 85).

The point to be made about "Death in the Desert" is its similarity to the kind of art Agee told Father Flye he wanted to create:

> *I'd like, in a sense, to combine what Chekhov did with what Shakespeare did—that is, to move from the dim, rather eventless beauty of C. to huge geometric plots such as Lear. And to make this transition without its seeming ridiculous. And to do the whole so that it flows naturally, and yet, so that the whole— words, emotion, characters, situation, etc.—has a discernible symmetry and a very definite* musical *quality—inaccurately speaking—I want to* write *symphonies. That is, characters introduced quietly (as are themes in a symphony, say) will recur in new lights, with new verbal orchestration, will work into counterpoint and get a sort of monstrous grinding beauty—and so on.* [Letters, p. 47]

The manner in which the narrator of "Death in the Desert" moves from the self-consciousness of his own pain to a cynical indifference and finally to a callous, personal resolution parallels the symphonic form described in this letter. Furthermore, the attitudes themselves are suggestive of a cold-bloodedness in the face of experience which, Agee felt, was necessary for a writer. In this regard the story becomes a confession and moral indictment of himself as an artist, revealing the frustrating tension between life and art that he experienced. Yet the narrator, unsuccessful though he is at recollecting emotions from childhood, does acknowledge that in the concatenation of impressions surrounding the story's climax, disciplined and impervious to morality, his thoughts had "assumed substance and shape." In a broader perspective, therefore, the story itself becomes an objective correlative to the artistic struggle: his mind must be as "quick and fluent" as the touring car bypassing the Negro. And of course, except for the luck that he is *in* the car, the hitchhiker he is bypassing might be himself.

The importance of this story is even more clearly revealed in the light of succeeding events. In the semester following its publication, the spring of 1931, I. A. Richards gave two courses at Harvard, both of which Agee attended. The effect was overwhelming: "his power over people was extravagant," Agee told Father Flye, "and almost unlimited. Everyone who knew him was left in a clear, tingling daze. "(*Letters*, p. 53). Specifically, Agee was hard put to define what had taken place; but by comparing their writings at the time, it is reasonable to assume that Richards merely qualified and expanded ideas Agee already had begun to develop. For instance, since Agee wanted to devise "a poetic diction that will cover the whole range of events" (*Letters*, p. 48), it is not difficult to imagine his receptivity to Richards's teaching on poetic diction. In *Science and Poetry,* a tract published in 1926 and revised in 1935, Richards had written that a poet works with the "full body" of words—with, that is, essentially their denotative as well as connotative significance, which reflects "the whole meaning of the words as the printed signs cannot."[3] This sort of psychological scrutiny of semantics, which was the thrust of Richards's writing and teaching during the mid-1920s and early 1930s, was undeniably eye-opening to the young Romantic poet who was trying to establish an organic relationship between word and thing. In *Principles of Literary Criticism* (1924) and *Practical Criticism, A Study of Literary Judgment* (1929), Richards had analyzed what led up to and away from the fact of a poem, the way in which experience was acquired, and the way in which its poetic representation was understood. But his discussion of the intellectual and emotional effects of poetic language and the way in which that language refers to a specific set of needs, stirs a

A Portrait of the Artist as a Young Man

specific set of impulses, and develops corresponding thoughts and attitudes in a reader—that might be considered an effort to train the tools of modern psychology on Wordsworth's "Preface to the Second Edition" of the *Lyrical Ballads.* Considering Richards' enormous effect on Agee, there is a stream of continuity here which cannot be overlooked.

In the process of defining poetry as a "spontaneous overflow of powerful feelings," Wordsworth described the manner in which an experience is translated into a poem:

> *For our continued influxes of feeling are modified and directed by our thoughts, which are indeed the representatives of all our past feelings; and, as by contemplating the relation of these general representatives to each other, we discover what is really important to men, so, by the repetition and continuance of this act, our feelings will be connected with important subjects, till at length, if we be originally possessed of much sensibility, such habits of mind will be produced that, by obeying blindly and mechanically the impulses of these habits, we shall describe objects, and utter sentiments, of such a nature, and in such connection with each other, that the understanding of the reader must necessarily be in some degree enlightened, and his affections strengthened and purified.[4]*

This process of accommodating feelings to habits of mind so that they might be described "blindly and mechanically" is simply expanded in relation to language by Richards:

> *The experience itself, the tide of impulses sweeping through the mind, is the source and sanction of the words. They represent this experience itself, not any set of perceptions or reflections, though often to a reader who approaches the poem wrongly they will seem to be only a series of remarks about other things. But to a suitable reader the words—if they actually spring from experience and are not due to verbal habits, to the desire to be effective, to factitious excogitation, to imitation, to irrelevant contrivances, or to any other of the failings which prevent most people*

from writing poetry—the words will reproduce in his mind a simi-
lar play of interests putting him for the while into a similar situa-
*tion and leading to the same response. [*Science and Poetry, *p. 35]*

Taken together, the two passages describe the same Romantic
strategy: that the poet must accommodate himself to experience
in such a way that he will translate it spontaneously and accurately into language. It is, of course, the question of the medium,
of language, which Richards opened like a Pandora's box for
Agee. Significantly, the process of this Romantic strategy and
Agee's particular difficulty with it was the subject of his last piece
of fiction published in the May 1931 *Advocate* (117:9–24), the
three-section story "They That Sow in Sorrow Shall Reap."

The narrator, a young man working construction during his
vacation from Harvard, is living in a clean, well-lighted New England boarding house. The first part of the story takes place
around the evening meal, after which the narrator is proposi-
tioned by his landlady's husband. The third part of the story
concerns a muscular young worker whom the narrator brings to
the boarding house and who, seeing another proposition made,
beats the old man and the narrator who tries to intervene. The
story ends as the narrator tries to sum up his feelings and those of
his landlady and her husband over the incident. However, it is the
middle section of the story which is the most significant. This is
actually a soliloquy by the narrator concerning his attempt to
write the story. "The mind," he tells the reader, "is rarely audience to experience in perfection"; for experience, as a rule, "is
broken upon innumerable sharp irrelevancies":

their rhythms are so subtly involved, so misgoverned by chance,
as to be beyond analysis; and the living mind, that must endure
and take part, is soon fugitive before, or else, however brave, falls
*to pieces beneath this broad unbeautiful pour of chaos. [*Prose,
pp. 93–94]

At this point Agee reminds the reader that "the experience re-

35
A Portrait
of the Artist
as a Young
Man

ferred to is objective; the same difficulties hold in the case of subjective experience" (*Prose*, p. 94). Then he complicates his observation:

> *The true sum of experience is, as a rule, an inconceivably complex interpenetration of subjective and objective experience. And the true sum and whole of experience is doubly chaotic.* [Prose, p. 94]

But Agee's narrator is not merely complaining of the difficulty of combining two traditions of Romantic aesthetics: the English, with its emphasis on the subjective self, and the American, with its emphasis on objective reality. More particularly, he is discussing a profound personal dilemma. That the mind has only two alternatives in the face of experience—either to flee, as "Death in the Desert" suggests, or to be overwhelmed, as the soliloquy indicates—is to expose the emotional dichotomy at the base of Agee's temperament. Clearly his sensitivity to the immediacy of reality could debilitate him as an artist. The impetus for his later poem "A Chorale," in which he rails against the misuse of God's creation, can certainly be attributed to this sensitivity—as can the entire volume of *Permit Me Voyage*, which is dedicated to the service of God. But what he had sought as an artistic defense, recalling the experience of "Death in the Desert"—"a mood of sustained callousness and irony which I thought one desert afternoon had perpetuated in me" (*Prose*, p. 94)—is also susceptible to another sensitivity:

> . . . *when I attempt to make real use of these instruments of perception, I realize two things: my own weakness and diffuseness of mind, and the fearful unarrangement of life realized with such completeness and sincerity as my mind may be capable of* [Prose, p. 94]

The soliloquy, then, is more than an illustration of the difficulty of assimilating experience, for the narrator tries to understand the momentary variations of experience in an attempt to duplicate the kind of music it appears to be. Realizing that while he is recollecting his relationship to the germinal experience that relationship has changed, he sets down the problem:

I have tried to work out to my own satisfaction, some aspects of the mind's reaction to experience. I have tried to match this reaction with the patterns of music; the idea is incongruous....

Yet, from time to time, I am aware of a definite form and rhythm and melody of existence: however fluctuate and intermittent its progress may be, it is a progress; out of long, contrapuntal passages of tantalizing and irreconcilable elements there emerges sometimes an enormous clear chord. And at that moment—or, rather, through its reverberations in our brain, the whole commonplaceness of existence is transfigured—becomes monstrously powerful, and beautiful, and significant—assuming these qualities validly but unanswerably—, and descends through tangled discords, once more into commonplaceness, with nothing answered, nothing gained, and heaven undisturbed. [Prose, pp. 96-97]

37
A Portrait
of the Artist
as a Young
Man

If he had written nothing else, this passage alone would adequately represent the complexity of James Agee's early sensibility. At its basis there is the Romantic impulse, the writer's interest in the relationship of the mind to experience and of the relationship of the senses to deeper values. In the latter, the "reverberations in our brain," there is a definition of the perspective from which Agee later wrote *Let Us Now Praise Famous Men*. "I suppose the essentials of which this music is compounded," he writes, "are the facts as they are, tempered by sternness and pity and calm" (*Prose*, p. 97). This definition, almost echoing Richards's analysis of cognition—"Signs on the retina, taken up by a set of needs" (*Science and Poetry*, p. 29)—was hardly altered for *Famous Men*: "You share a naturalist's regard for the 'real,' " he wrote, "but have this regard for it on a plane which in your mind brings it level in value at least to music and poetry" (*FM*, p. 238). It is, however, the realization of the perspective in language which is most threatening. In the climax of the story, in prose most closely resembling Faulkner's both in rhythm and intention, Agee tries to translate his experience into "Word Music":

38

A Portrait
of the Artist
as a Young
Man

> *Grafton stood in quiet; then drew away, and with flat palm*
> *struck across the mouth the old man, who, mouth flashing blood,*
> *for an instant assumed in all amazement the Jeffries sparring*
> *stance, with amazement gone raised supplicating tiny hands like a*
> *Moslem mole, while, face all blood and streaming tears, he shrank*
> *among the sorrowing flowers of morning bitterly crying, and with*
> *dependent hands fluttering before head;*
>
> *while boarders rose from their chairs and looked in amaze and*
> *impended to interfere, then drew back and quickly, but staring*
> *back, removed from the porch and roomward made kind haste;*
>
> *and two across the street stopped to stare;*
>
> *and a second time the boy raised lowered arm through an arc*
> *and with flat palm struck through hands the old man's mouth;*
> *who, bawling abominable brat, splayed evening with weeping;*
>
> *while with crashed plate and rushing footsteps—murderous*
> *anger moving me with all strength I struck the boy, behind the*
> *ear; he turned and dealt upon my cheekbone his fist and power,*
> *that with split skin and shrouded purpose I sank against wall and*
> *floor, Defender of What?* [Prose, pp. 105-06]

The passage is an attempt at reporting and responding simultane-
ously. By removing articles and possessive pronouns, yet retaining
images and metaphors, Agee makes his words name objects at the
same time that he evaluates them. In this way each paragraph
retains a photographic quality, and the juxtaposition of the paragraphs resembles a series of jump cuts or the staccato chords of a
symphonic climax. Agee had used this ultimately musical device
in writing the climax of "Death in the Desert," but at that time
he had not yet developed the persona who is both writer and
reader. For Agee's narrator's soliloquy concerns not merely the
difficulty of assimilating experience or the impression of "a definite form and rhythm and melody of existence," but inevitably
the premise that experience is ill served by being presented in
language, that by putting words on a page the writer is encourag-
ing an experience entirely separate from the one about which he
writes. In order to satisfy the tensions of this separation, Agee has
created a biofocal persona, a participant in the narration as well

as a narrator of the participation, who fills the gap between the experience of the writer and the experience of the reader. Realizing the inadequacy of language and the devices of fiction to truly communicate the constituents of the experience, Agee's persona, eventually the narrator of *Let Us Now Praise Famous Men,* is a moving center besieged by information, attempting to account for the consistent variances between the subject and the object.

39

*A Portrait
of the Artist
as a Young
Man*

There are too many ways of overlooking this accomplishment. Durrant Da Ponte has stated that Agee had "no clear idea of who he was or where his talents lay." Robert Bingham claims that Agee was intimidated "by the role he had written for himself as a 'really great writer.'" A *Time* critic suggested that he was "often rendered impotent by the severity of his own dedication." And John Updike believes that "the private game of translating life into language . . . did not sufficiently fascinate him."[5] But the fact of the matter is that James Agee was complex enough as an individual, and tormented enough by that complexity, to write one very original work of art. He wrote many other things besides *Famous Men,* each of which sheds some light on the chaos of contemporary life, but it is a masterpiece he is pursuing in the writing of "They That Sow," and he pursues it until the end of the decade. If, therefore, the work to follow seems tangential; if Agee seems to be a stronger prose writer than he is a poet but insists on writing poetry; if he is really a better naturalist than he is a Romantic but insists on being a Romantic—then it must be remembered that this young man, like Thoreau and Melville before him, was in pursuit of some vast yet confused ambition of himself and that, in the words of his own soliloquy concerning experience, "however fluctuate and intermittent its progress may be, it *is* a progress."

It is November or December 1932, perhaps three o'clock in the morning. On the fifty-second floor of the Chrysler Building, tucked away in a corner of the offices of *Fortune* magazine, in a cubicle cluttered with coffee cups and dirty ashtrays, James Agee is writing:

> . . . *behind the line of weaves these belts converge into an alternation of colors as regular as that of notes on a piano keyboard. Each "tooth" in the reed holds three yarns, and these hundreds of yarns have no more relation to pattern than a silent keyboard has to a fugue. The crucial matter of playing the fugue, of selecting the colors is accomplished at the very crest of the loom.* ["Sheep and Shuttleworths," Fortune 7(January 1933):45]

Schiller's "Ode to Joy," its arpeggios counterpointed with the orchestral score of the final movement of Beethoven's Ninth Symphony, sounds from the phonograph. The pale light and puny sound thrust barely into the body of night beyond the office windows, and the planes and contours of the city of New York swim beneath the depths of the American Great Depression.

It is impossible to recreate the atmosphere of those months. The details of the scene above suggest something of the context of James Agee's life at the time he began to work for *Fortune*. The peculiar relationship of art to life, of Beethoven to the Chrysler Building, of the fugue to the loom, was not quite that of a flower to a charnel house. In the 1920s, Hart Crane and Vachel Lindsay had sung the glories of modern and technological America, endorsing the energy and vision that had transformed the continent. By April 1932, however, both men had committed suicide. The optimism which had prevailed through the boom years and early months of the Crash was beginning to wane. One-fifth of the schoolchildren of New York City were undernourished. Almost fifteen million people were out of work. Demonstrations were taking place in major cities. Farmers, though inured to years of hard times, were revolting in the countryside. In mid-August in New York, after having contemplated suicide because (as he told Father Flye), "I simply am not capable of being the kind of person, doing the kinds of things, which I want to be" (*Letters*, p. 57), Agee was moved to comment, "The whole spiritual *tone* of this time seems the darkest and saddest in centuries" (*Letters*, p. 58).

Our appreciation of this tone—a settling into despair—depends somewhat on our ability to comprehend the scope and complexity of the preceeding decade. Elements that amounted to unprecedented decadence, that prompted Agee to "account for Elizabethan extravagances in 1930 life" (letter to Macdonald, May? 1932), are commonplace today: unqualified credit, conspicuous consumption, and the deliberate creation by advertisers of a dream life to further the rapidly expanding economy. An even more poignant irony lies in the fact that the determination expressed by Agee in 1928, to avoid Babylon's advertising and brokerage, was by 1932 considered a luxury; Robert Fitzgerald has written, "If a freshman in '29 could feel confined by the university, in '32 it seemed a confinement all too desirable by contrast with what lay ahead" (*Memoir*, p. 15). It is therefore easily understandable that when Dwight Macdonald wrote to Agee shortly before graduation to offer him a job as a staff writer for the three-year-old *Fortune* magazine, Agee replied quickly. He received, he said, the contents of Macdonald's letter "with eyes rolling upward & stomach downward for joy, relief, gratitude and such things" (May? 1932).

Agee was undoubtedly somewhat naive in his expectations. He was genuinely fascinated with the publishing world. On April 24, 1929, when Macdonald had begun working with Luce, Agee had written him:

. . . your connection with Time *is fresh and most satisfying news. What sort of work do you do?—or does a member of the*

staff do any and every sort of thing? I'd like to follow up your work, if that is possible.

Hence when the *Fortune* offer came through, there is no reason to doubt his excitement: "Besides the fairly fundamental fact that I don't want to starve," he told his friend—probably in May 1932—"there are dozens of other reasons I want *uh* job and many more why I am delighted to get this one."

Unfortunately, though typically for 1932, he was soon overcome by despair. Perhaps he had not realized the difficulty of getting started. Perhaps he had not accounted for the extreme demands of the work. Perhaps he had not understood the pervasiveness of the Depression. Whatever the reason, the flippancy with which he had satirized *la vie bohéme* in his Harvard take-off on Marlowe, "The Passionate Poet to his Love," was blasted in his exposure to New York in the summer of 1932. Published in the *Advocate* in February, the poem is an audacious proposition to a young lady to be "Wife, mother or nonentity" to "guard the Inception of the Word" (*Poems*, pp. 137–38, ll. 10, 18). Yet Agee's second letter from New York to Father Flye speaks with deep compassion of girls "ruined in love by the grinding of old conventions to which they've been trained, against new conventions which they honestly feel compelled to live by" (*Letters*, p. 59). It is more than likely that he was experiencing the same conflict himself, the witty idealism of Harvard meeting the grinding misery of New York. Ending his letter, he speaks of a vague yet painful reaction which expressed itself two ways:

> . . . *of a love and pity and joy that nearly floors you, and the other of Swift's sort, when you see the people you love—any mob of them in this block I live in—with a tincture of sickness and cruelty and selfishness in the faces of most of them, sometimes an apparently total and universal blindness to kindliness and good and beauty. You have a feeling that they could never be cured and that all effort is misspent—and then you also know the generations of training in pain that have made the evil in them, and know it would be more than worth dying for* [Letters, p. 61]

The love-hate ambivalence in these sentences was symptomatic of his personal despair ("I simply am not capable of being the kind of person, doing the kinds of things, which I want to be"), but the last sentence of this passage is the most revealing. After an apparent realization that his despair is based on a fear that his efforts are misspent, he apprehends the egotism of such feelings and remembers, almost parenthetically, that it was for these sins Christ had died, and that, correspondingly, he should be willing to make an equivalent sacrifice.

In one respect writing articles on rugs and strawberries and railroad terminals and baldness does not seem to have bothered Agee half so much as did this moral sensitivity to the needs of others. He told Father Flye, "the only writing I do which approaches decency is on this job" (*Letters*, p. 56), and the assessment is accurate for several reasons. The early work he did for *Fortune* was imbued with a mordant enthusiasm; he was obviously enjoying the task. For instance, following his article on rugs, Agee wrote "The Third Favorite Flavor," a piece about strawberries. Its opening paragraph is a masterpiece of understatement.

In England, behind walls of a respectable age, strawberries are still served at Solemn High Tea. In England this June the school tuckshop will be clamorous with hard-hatted little Harrovians absorbing "dringers," a somewhat lily-gilding mixture of fresh strawberries and strawberry ice cream. In England there are still shops where, for sixpence, you can eat whole shoals of berries beached high in Devonshire cream—as many as you can down but none to take away. There the season is short and berries are picked as berries should be, fully ripe, red on the plant. There, as throughout Europe, some berries still carry that faint tang of pine which sets them above the rest of their race. There they are eaten with true relish and a certain quiet reverence, for in England strawberries still play their part in a great tradition and few polite novelists can forget it. [Fortune 7(April 1933):64]

In this paragraph Agee is certainly taking advantage of his reader's particular prejudice against the English to lay a thin veneer over the real object of his attack, the patrons of Voisin's and the Ritz-Carlton, whose epicurism in spite of worldwide hunger was exceeded only by their failure to see themselves beneath the satirist's depiction. A 1931 housing law or the Cincinnati railroad terminal brought forth less inspired prose; nor did Agee have the necessary knowledge of economics to explicate the consequences of the quinine cartels or of the international speculators, about which he wrote. But when he could work his subject around to a moral evaluation, he had a leverage upon his sensibility.

This intent is implicit in all his *Fortune* articles and is clearly revealed in the following fragment found among his papers, a memo most probably written out of frustration and never sent.

> *It is possible to speak of Art For Art's Sake. It is not possible to speak of Business wholly for Business's Sake. All that has been discussed as Business ceases, at a certain clearly definable point, to be relevant to that kind of discussion. [Insert: For at the moment the good reaches the ultimate consumer,] it ceases to be measured in business terms. It has become an intimate and shaping part of the substance of life, and we are bound to be more interested in quality than in quantity; to discuss questions of value that cannot be answered either by Bureaus of Standards or by [bargain counters?].* [1]

The statement is consistent with the intentions—formulated in the soliloquy of "They That Sow" and eventually consummated in *Let Us Now Praise Famous Men*—to respond to what has been reported. In tracing this American journalistic tradition from Stephen Crane's "The Open Boat" through Hemingway's *The Green Hills of Africa* to Truman Capote's *In Cold Blood*, William Wiegand has defined it as "the capacity to universalize the implication of an isolated real happening." [2] Had *Fortune* allowed Agee to satisfy this need in his work, it is questionable whether he would have considered journalism an infringement upon his time. For, quite simply, his struggle to reclaim his creativity in the face of his evolving career as a commercial writer grew out of a peculiar emotional syndrome: he had to sacrifice his poetry in order to earn money to live; but if he were freed of economic demands, he feared, he would have to sacrifice his moral obligation to others in order to write poetry. At Harvard he had expressed the same dilemma. In "A Poem of Poets" he defined the duty of the poet "to do thankful honor to Him" who gave the poet life and inspiration (*Poems*, p. 134, l. 14). But by making poetry an instrument of God in the same way that he wished to make journalism an instrument of morality, Agee could reduce the tension between the amoral perspective of the artist and the moral perspective of the saint. The effort was doomed to failure, however, not only because of human imperfection, but also because of the unspeakable glory of God. Thus he ended the poem in a frustrated rage, concluding that the poet's egotistical motivation led him

To crown the mind with fame, and God with earthbound passion,
Flaw truth with beauty, make a holy whore of sickened love;
Once more, and now forever, impends that immolation
Whence we shall rise to damn still other poets with half-blind
    power. [Poems, p. 135, ll. 24–27]

A mood such as this probably led Agee to conceive the subject of what would be his longest narrative poem, the Byronic "John Carter," a life story of "the typical American Young Man . . . an orthodox Roman Catholic devil, God-given to the world, a New Messiah of Evil" (*Poems*, p. 79). It is not important that, to all intents and purposes, the poem is a failure. There is evidence that Agee realized this months before he wrote the above sentences in application for a Guggenheim fellowship in late October 1932. In the same letter in which he thanked Macdonald for the *Fortune* offer he had mentioned working on a "new somewhat cockeyed narrative poem," parts of which were appearing in the June 1932 *Advocate:*

The poetry is, on the whole, a flop, but I'm fool enough to have faith in the idea: vaguely that I can take a somewhat stock bawdy situation, fit it to characters common to Chaucer & to midwestern "realistic" novels,—and make something of it Chaucer

at best wouldn't vomit on. Only it would seem to take practice,
very careful study, and about 10 times the talent & 5 times the
guts I have, to do it.

What matters are Agee's intentions of leaving the country for France and of writing nothing short of an American epic, establishing "a widespread popular awareness of the prevailing validity of religious faith and of artistic morality as opposed to 'scientific morality' . . . In short," as he told the Guggenheim committee, "to help to change (if it can be changed) the prevalent negative state of mind into a positive state" (*Poems,* p. 80).

Like many of the projects he would later outline in letters and notebooks, these proposals have a grandiose and windy quality that undoubtedly led the committee to reject them. They nevertheless do contain, as does the poem, the themes of Agee's approaching artistic maturity. He wished, for instance, to establish the validity not only of religious faith, but also of artistic morality, so that he would be able to assuage the guilt over his vocation. Undoubtedly the impulse was very much responsible for the publication two years later of *Permit Me Voyage.* Though it is treated only superficially in "John Carter," the poem is revealing in other ways. For instance, the following twelve lines indicate a good deal about the state of his talent in 1932:

Homer and Plato and the dirt are one
Shakespeare and Swift inform the deathstruck flower;
The wild black breadth of Russia's but begun
To rear its green illimitable power;
Our Western Zero shrewdly chokes our sun:
Yet, in this brief and steeply shadowed hour
Ere flesh deserts and earth adopts the bone
There's more to do than sit and make sweet moan.

The piebald earth revolves and still the rain
Silverly stoops on tower and field and hill;
Still man is man and still the man-wrought pain
Is studious to hurt and waste and kill.

[Poems, p. 91, ll. 313–25]

In two preceding stanzas Agee had introduced a transition between a criticism of contemporary American poets and poetry and a depiction of the country that follows. In one sense the first line is an excuse for the satire to follow; that is, the American reader will not take it any more seriously than he takes Plato or dirt. In another sense it is an equation of works of art with matters of life. As if to test the cogency of this statement, however, Agee puts aside his crude satiric persona. The verse takes a sudden and serious turn when contemporary social issues are rejected in favor of more universal literary themes. At this point the poet's concentration can be seen to improve. Compare, for instance, the vague "green illimitable power," the incongruent matching of "deserts" and "adopts," with the persistent *st's* and coordinate phrasing of the second stanza. This is prelude to a counterpointed treatment of two of Agee's favorite metaphors, sunrise and harvest, which he had made the framework of the "Epithalamium" and which also furnished the subject of "Theme and Variations," a poem begun—according to Robert Fitzgerald's conjecture—upon Agee's return from a *Fortune* assignment to Tennessee in the summer of 1933. The earlier mention of "Epithalamium" suggested that Agee's preference for the diurnal metaphor began at Exeter with his reading of Virgil. Although the device is found in Archibald MacLeish's "You, Andrew Marvell," which appeared in 1930, the same year as "Epithalamium," it is doubtful MacLeish's poem influenced Agee in his conception. Rather, the use of this diurnal metaphor in both poems arises out of a contemporary perspective shared by Agee and MacLeish—a comparison of the cosmic proportions of history, geography and the changes of season with the prosaic yet concrete efforts of man. There is no doubt, however, that by 1933 Agee had read the MacLeish poem. He had entitled one of his Harvard short stories "You, Andrew Volstead," and MacLeish was a good friend on the staff at *Fortune*. It is also quite probable that both poets were influenced, as was Hart Crane, by the "aerial perspectives" advocated by the verticalist group at *transition* magazine.[3]

Whatever Agee's various influences, a comparison of sections of these poems in which he uses the diurnal metaphor, particularly with attention to the use of diction and rhythm, suggests the real strengths and weaknesses of Agee's young talent. Unlike Mac-Leish, who describes the sun's noon and receding shadow from a subjective point of view, Agee narrates the sunset, counterpointing it with the harvest in "John Carter" and "Theme and Variations" and with the act of love in "Epithalamium," which opens as follows:

*Now day departs: Upreared the darkness climbs
The breathless sky, leans wide above the fields,
And snows its silence round the muttering chimes:
The night is come that bride to bridegroom yields.*

[Poems, p. 29, ll. 1-4]

The sunrise section of "John Carter" follows:

*This breadth of earth is crumpled into stone
    On east and west, and broad on either hand
Two seas are spread, and on the east alone
    The daybreak leans and soon will find the land:
The gleaming looms of gloomy brine are grown
    Sure in the light, and now discovered stand
Islands and toiling ships and the long shore
Fire-born, sea-suckled now and evermore.*

[Poems, p. 92, ll. 337-44]

Both passages exhibit almost too much activity, especially "Epithalamium," where the darkness is "upreared" and "climbs" the "breathless" sky, then "leans wide" and "snows . . . round . . . muttering chimes." The problem is alleviated somewhat in "John Carter" by the consistent horizontal terminology—"breadth," "broad," "spread," and "leans"—as well as by the more prosaic syntax. But in both poems Agee overworks the diction, cluttering the verse to give a rich aural quality to spite the action. In contrast, the simplicity of "Theme and Variations" is unusual. The first three stanzas, stating the theme, read:

Night stands up the east:
Day glides down the west:
Lax in his fur the beast
The bird with brow in breast

Yields each the addled hope
That stood him sunward guide:
Through all the shadow's scope
The dew distends its tide:

And all is strifeless quite:
All free from all affray
And down the west falls night:
And up the east fares day:

[Poems, p. 53, ll. 1–12]

Here Agee relies upon declaration and image, giving the impression that the phenomenon is deeply felt and can be precisely expressed. The simple rhyme scheme, almost whispered in the first stanza and endowed with remarkable sotto voce in the third stanza by variation of the *a* vowel delicately balanced on the *f*'s, conveys the quiet musicality of night. Aside from the stressed consonants of the second stanza, the poem is almost effortless in its realization, a fine marriage of form and content which Agee seldom realized in verse.

In fact, those qualities which are most often mentioned in praise of Agee's poetry—"a masterly control of rhythms," "a delicate and perceptive ear"—as MacLeish notes in his "Foreword" to *Permit Me Voyage* (p. 7)—though genuine strengths of his talent, were worked more favorably in his prose. The opening sentences of his 1933 piece on the Tennessee Valley Authority are one example.

The Tennessee River system begins on the worn magnificent crests of the southern Appalachians, among the earth's older mountains, and the Tennessee River shapes its valley into the form of a boomerang, bowing it to its sweep through seven states. Near Knoxville the streams still fresh from the mountain are linked and thence the master stream spreads the valley most

*richly southward, swims past Chattanooga and bends down into
Alabama to roar like blown smoke through the floodgates of
Wilson Dam, to slide becalmed along the crop-cleansed fields of
Shiloh, to march due north across the high diminished plains of
Tennessee and through Kentucky spreading marshes toward the
valley's end.* ["The Project is Important," Fortune *8 (October
1933):81]*

In these sentences Agee employs the musical quality of the words
and phrases to a purpose. Freed of the constriction imposed by
poetic meter, the full effect or "body" of a word lends the sentence a rhythm it does not already possess. The quadrisyllabic
"magnificent" arrests the reader precisely—Agee suggests—as the
crests of the Appalachians would. The coupling of "boomerang,
bowing," followed by the four sibilants of "sweep through seven
states," gives the sense of a momentarily knotted, suddenly released sluice of water. Although comparisons between the nature
of poetry and prose inevitably fail for want of definition, the
temptation to create effects is often fatal to a poet where it is an
asset to a prose writer, for prose allows a looser construction than
does poetry. This circumstance certainly affected Agee's attempts
at creating "Word Music." For the remainder of the 1930s Agee's
poetry was almost solely an experiment in musical rhythms and
sounds. When it relied on traditional forms, Robert Fitzgerald has
written, a "crudity and callowness came back into the verse rhythms, as though rhyming were now . . . only doodling in the mar-
gins of his prose" (*Poems,* p. xi). Only once does Agee betray any
awareness of his limited ability as a poet. In his first letter from
New York to Father Flye, when he was on the brink of suicide,
he wrote that "poetry is the product of adolescence—or of an
emotionally adolescent frame of mind: and that as this state of
mind changes, poetry is likely to dry up" (*Letters,* p. 56). Otherwise, as Fitzgerald suggests in his "Memoir," he was convinced of
his vocation as a poet and an artist. The two were synonymous;
without poetry, where could he turn?

Something of a crisis came in October 1933, and the consequences are worth noting:

In the first place we have no money and I must earn a living. In the second, beyond that necessity I care very little about my job, except for my own writing and whatever may help me in it. In the third, the editor-in-chief was much impressed by my Tennessee Valley story . . . and this morning called me and talked to me. [Letters, p. 66]

What follows in this letter to Father Flye is a complex network of desires and frustrations, hopes and illusions:

He was as honest and as swell as anyone could wish for: my story was one of the best pieces of writing he'd ever seen in Fortune, *but he knew I am weak on organization and that I understand business very poorly. On the strength of my usefulness as a writer, he is willing for me to stay on: but naturally on certain conditions: He will feed me tough business stories thick and fast: I must do my best to learn the business ropes: they shan't expect anything wildly fast out of me, but the idea is this: that I really am interested in doing well with this job: in making it a part of my career.* [Letters, p. 66]

Agee blames no one. Luce is "as honest and as swell as anyone could wish for." His own writing is good, and he feels it in the straight declaration of Luce's compliment. But beneath the transparency of the jaded rhetoric is his simple desire to succeed. Speaking of his work for *Fortune* in a letter to Fitzgerald, he called his feelings about it a "hard masochistic liking without enthusiasm or trust" ("Memoir," p. 20). But it was simply one more cruel paradox that he would find himself in some degree dependent on the satisfaction of his work at a time when he wanted to be independent of its demands. Writing to his fellow poet Fitzgerald, he could say, "the fault, dear *Fortune*, is in me: that I hate any job on earth" ("Memoir," p. 20). But to his father confessor he was obliged to lay down his nagging suspicion: "If I had as much confidence about writing as I have intention, everything might be much easier" (*Letters*, p. 67). Out of the ambivalence of this fear and anger he struggled to confirm his idea of himself as an artist. Following the rejection of his Guggenheim application, he thought of writing a collection of short stories. But eventually, as Fitzgerald relates, he brought together what he considered his best poems and submitted them to the Yale University Press.

The volume, which appeared in October 1934 in the distinguished Yale Younger Poets series, has been amply criticized.[4] The poems do not differ greatly in quality from those already discussed. Contemporary critical reactions—and MacLeish's "Foreword" is typical—were lukewarm.[5] Recently critics have chiefly mentioned three of the poems: the prose poem "Dedication," "A Chorale," and the title lyric, "Permit Me Voyage." The irony that the most obvious statements of Agee's religious intent are becoming known after thirty years is somewhat explained by Fitzgerald's comment:

At twenty-five, after two years in New York, he published an openly religious book of poems. MacLeish was not alone in ignoring what it said; the reviewers also ignored it. It was as if the interests and pressures of the time made it inaudible. ["Memoir," p. 27]

Nevertheless Agee was aware of the times and of the probable reaction to his verse. He sought to explain it to himself in his "Reflections on *Permit Me Voyage*." Though at first it seems he intended publish this commentary on the volume, he wisely decided against such a course. He wrote that the collection contained "such things as seem to me, for one reason or another, finished, crystalized, behind me." However, "Dedication," "A Chorale," and "Permit Me Voyage" were all written in 1934; and if they are reflective, they are also contemporaneous, written out of the motives and needs of the present as well as the past. Perhaps the real clue to the irrelevance of the volume can be found in these three poems, revealing that the themes of the collection were the result of a terrifying personal urgency, of a need to define the self in relation to itself rather than in relation to others.

"Permit Me Voyage," the title poem which closes the volume, is a case in point. It is reminiscent of "A Poem of Poets," in which Agee had defined the artistic vocation as an instrument of God. In "Permit Me Voyage" he goes a step further and defines art as a means of salvation for himself and for the race. For although his "heart and mind discharted lie," his "flesh is priestly stole" (*Poems*, p. 49, ll. 3, 8),

Whence forth shall my heart and mind
To God through soul entirely bow.

[Poems, *p. 50, ll. 9–10]*

At this point in the poem he repeats condemnations also found in "A Chorale":

I know in this gigantic day
What God is ruined and I know
How labors with Godhead this day.

[ll. 14–16]

However, the poet implies, the nature of evil besetting his time is no more specific than man's desecration of the Creator's love, and the poet's role is no more specific than to serve God as His herald to preserve the race—for which he prays: "Permit me voyage, Love, into your hands" (l. 25).

Although the poem is flawed by strained rhythms and wrenched syntax (though not so much as others in the collection), it is summation. Agee saw its parallel in "Dedication." "An obligatory job," he noted of both, and it is clear that he did not use the term idly. Although he sought the "generalized and impersonal tone of the Litany or General Supplication" ("Reflections"), "Dedication" is closer to the stridency of the Old Testament prophets, Jeremiah and Isiah. Of the poem, Agee wrote:

I knew very well that such a dedication would be impossible to
write worthily. I knew very well too, that such a dedication, to
people who have never been able to dedicate themselves to so
much as the hole between the knees of their women, would seem
obscenely pretentious. I knew that if you dedicated yourself hon-
estly as you could to all things as you loved and detested them,
you would be making a damned fool of yourself, and a prize

target. I also knew that such a dedication was the least a human being could do; that it would be a confusion of the personal and the general; and that in my weakness and ignorance, I could not succeed in giving it serenity, and would have to do as I might (which was poorly) with solemnity. And finally I knew that as a would-be poet, it was an absolutely obligatory job, and that it should have to appear in this first book. So I wrote it. ["Reflections"]

Hence the obligation was moral, a means of giving value to "all things as you loved and detested them" by subsuming them under the prophetic mission he conceived as poetry. This "Dedication" nevertheless exhibits a desperate air of contrivance. As Agee had noted, his Hebraic injunctions—"Of these merchants and of these rulers may the loins thaw with a shrieking pain, and may there be slow nails in the skulls of each" (*Poems*, p. 11)—are without serenity. Similarly, the love for those "who in all times have sought truth and who have told it in their art or in their living, who died in honor; and chiefly to these: Christ: Dante: Mozart" (*Poems*, p. 8) is overly solemn. One is excoriation, the other litany; neither is assumed from a deep love, but rather from fear on the one hand and adulation on the other. This dual tone supports the early line of "Permit Me Voyage": "My heart and mind discharted lie." And the closing line of that poem—"Permit me voyage, Love, into your hands"—bears a close relationship to the spirit of the "Dedication":

It was to indicate that love was meant in the, oh well, in the Dantesque sense. But it also includes, critics will please to observe, every degree of love down to the love of the hatred of the agony of eating breakfast when scarcely awake. ["Reflections"]

This confusion between loves and hates, the rationalization that hatreds are really loves, is, in fact, a confusion between the subject and objects of consciousness, pointed out by J. Douglas Perry.[6] This confusion, moreover, resides at the heart of Agee's personal life as well as of his writing throughout the 1930s. It prompted him to compare his gift copy of *Permit Me Voyage* to

Father Flye with the gesture of a dying man, passing out "his hair and his toenails to friends" (*Letters*, p. 68). Indeed, the religious commitment of the volume at times seems an attempt to rescue himself from his own confusion. He admitted to his spiritual father that

The wise answer of course would be that there is only one coordinator and guide, and that he is come at through self-negation. But: that can mean nothing to me until or unless I learn it for myself. Without scrupulousness I am damned forever, and my base, if I ever find it, must be of my own finding and understanding or it is no sort of base at all. [Letters, *p. 69*]

In succeeding letters he cast about for a more practical answer to his disorientation. On the same day he wrote the above, he fired off another letter to Father Flye, asking about a teaching job at St. Andrew's. A month later he mentioned the Yaddo artists' colony near Saratoga, New York. But by that time he had decided "to work hard enough not to care how or why [he was] living" (*Letters*, p. 73).

Of Agee's thoughts and work throughout the latter half of 1934 and 1935, Robert Fitzgerald has written well and quoted liberally. On the basis of such work as "The Great American Roadside," "The Drought," and "August in Saratoga" he was given a leave of absence from *Fortune*, beginning in November 1935. Eventually he and his wife Via went to Florida. But an indication that his conviction concerning his own writing had not changed in two years is his remark to Father Flye in September that he was considering spending the leave writing reviews for *Newsweek*. Another indication of deeper feelings is found in this paragraph:

Long's assassin was a brave man, but there were more deserving people to die killing. Hearst might head a purely local list but if you weren't being provincial about it I guess Hitler would nose him out. Hitler and several of his friends. I have thought how interesting and serviceable it would be to organize a group of terrorists: say 600 young men who don't care especially for their lives: to pair them off to trail the 300 key sonsofbitches of the earth (if they were that glibly easy to select): and exactly a year from then, at just the same hour all over the world, to ring up the assassinations. But I don't really qualify at all: I doubt it would do more good than harm: and you would certainly kill a good many innocent men, not all of them bystanders. [Letters, pp. 82-83]

Obviously Agee's vacation was coming none too soon. There was nowhere else for such gall to flow, unless inwardly, than into his writing. Perhaps a spirit such as this resulted, within the first few months of the vacation, in the bitter and nihilistic film sketch, "The House," his first piece of fiction since "They That Sow."

"The House: Notes for a moving picture" could have been started as early as the summer of 1935. It was published in 1937 by Horace Gregory in *New Letters in America.* Outside of comments in letters, "The House" is the first evidence of a renewed creative interest in film. His adaptation, not published until 1939, of a scene from André Malraux's *Man's Fate* probably dates from the same period. Both pieces, however, work with ideas for cinema which Agee had outlined in letters to Dwight Macdonald in the late 1920s. As Peter Ohlin has noted, the cinematic techniques found in "The House" were common to the films of the early 1930s. The sexual symbolism and brutality can be found in Buñuel and Dali (*Un Chien Andalou,* 1928 and *L'Age d'Or,* 1930), the anthropomorphism in Cocteau (*Le Sang d'un Poète,* 1930). Agee's use of montage was undoubtedly influenced by Eisenstein, and the still or meditative camera can be found in almost any film of the period. If there was a seminal influence, it was most likely René Clair's *Entr'acte* (1924), a film which anticipated the techniques of all these film makers and which Agee knew and admired. Nevertheless, many of the ideas Agee incorporated in the film were suggested by literature, as can be seen from this passage from his April 24, 1929 letter to Macdonald:

I'm trying to write a paper on the possibilities of the talkies— which I despise. Nevertheless, great things, (not in the movie manner) could be done with them. Both depend on the possibility of fusing pictures, sound, and in one case color, into a unity. One is—that they could be a fulfillment of all that Blake wanted to do—great pictures, poetry, color and music—the other is the chance they offer Joyce and his followers.

Both the opening and closing shots of "The House" are of "broad brilliant sunlit air . . . brought on with a plucked string of a cello on a high note." The closing shot inverts the cello sound "so that the resonance comes first; enlarges; and is sucked into the very abrupt pluck of sound into silence" (pp. 37, 55). These sounds and images are rhythmically spaced and held—the similarity to musical composition as well as to Agee's own poetry is obvious. There is no story. The film is made up of "events": a parade of fascisti boy scouts; a funeral procession of racing hearses; a recession of characters from an aged Victorian house; the theft of cut glass and silverware by the servants; a tour of the house, during which the camera discovers itself in a mirror; a rainstorm and flood which destroy the timepieces, the owner, and finally, the house itself; and a final scene in which poor children, playing in the lot where the house once stood, act out a funeral for a goldfish, seen earlier inside the house, and a wedding with cloth remnants from the house serving as the bridal veil. Thus the progress of the film is a descent through a nightmare into the imaginary games of children, counterpointed by sunlight, rain, and aftermath.

Seen in more concentrated focus, each "event" is actually self-destructive. The place of the action is "a middlesized provincial industrial city." A series of three carefully composed shots—taken from the center, left, and right of the main street in full sunlight—reveal incongruencies of detail. The street bisected by midday sun and shadow is deserted, but its neon signs are lit. Colored red and blue, they "spell out not real signwords but semi-intelligible or international names and nouns for suspense and disaster." From either side of the street a procession begins. First, "a legless pencil vendor . . . wearing a service tunic and an overseas cap," then two nuns who, lifting their faces to the camera reveal: "One, a doped and dangerous homosexualist. . . . The other, long hairy meeting brows . . . a swinging penis nose which, as it swings, discovers a lipless and chinless mouth" (pp. 37, 38, 39).

The remaining action is consistent with the surreal prologue: Agee's camera continues to discover fiends beneath the superficial respectability. Out of the marching boy scouts surrounding a float upon which stands a crucifix, "the basic position-one shot is crosslanced (not in double exposure) with swift intimate detail of childish feet grinding faces of Negroes, Jews." The crucifix in closer focus is "a stripped woman, handless and footless, nailed by her wrists and shins to the cross, whose lowered head . . . is a schoolboy globe of the earth. Above her head, in place of "Jesus of Nazareth, King of the Jews," is tacked the word MOTHER. Following the parade, a silence: "a loud, dry, empty and invisible whisk and clatter of applause," then: "within the brain of the camera . . . a gigantic bright black hearse blows from the lens . . . flying the stars and stripes" (pp. 39, 40). Moving from the funeral procession to the house itself, the camera pans over a number of disembodied arms lying on the ground, one bloodied, another holding a hammer, another a sickle, another artificial, another aged. The shot is duplicated in Agee's adaptation of *Man's Fate*, when the camera pans the mangled, wounded arms and heads of dying Communists awaiting execution.

The residents of the house, who have been suggested as the occupants of the hearses, are also grotesqueries: a man of sixty-five, "his face somewhat like that of the crueler photos of Harding"; a man of fifty, "upper half in executive, lower in golfing, costume"; "a heavy, fly-blown woman, his age," who wears a transparent dress, "beneath that her flesh squelched in a broad hard slippery girdle" upon which is a brooch of a "discolored and exhausted phallus"; a young man of thirty, "carrying a cocktail glass brimful of lightly fuming acid"; a young woman his age in a scanty bathing suit, carrying "a clear globe in whose center, sustained in alcohol, hangs a miniature foetus in a baby bonnet"; finally "an over-developed girl of nine, in traditionally white frilly party dress . . . submergedly desperate nympholeptic face." Behind them are the servants, "blank in face and in their tight gestures, completely but very flatly, deadly evil" (p. 42).

Following the recession of these characters from the house to a waiting car, the visual tone becomes decidedly more subtle. Rather than focusing on illusions that take shape before the camera, the perspective becomes documentary: the servants glance at the sky, their shoes cross the porch, the maid's hand undoes her apron bow. Objects are distorted by light: a fishbowl, a cut-glass punchbowl, lace curtains blown back by the wind. Mixing these techniques, as well as cutting back to the street scenes of the prologue, Agee commences a naturalistic portrait of the house itself. Shots, almost still in quality, from a number of angles, some slowly panning and holding, photographically reconstruct the house. Once the composite image is set, the camera begins to perceive flaws. Agee's instructions are as follows.

Everything should be strong, bright and arid, and each shot should be laid on square with a steady beat, not too slow though deliberate, not flashing (about two and a half seconds per rhythmic unit). Now, details of cracked paint blistered paint and of roofslates so close as at first to be unidentifiable: of painted nail-heads, of joined boards, of the wire hooks slates are hung by; closing with more extreme and now angled shots to establish the wicked angle of the ridged roof and its gables, fenced at every ridge with sharp iron lace; and with shots that fling this sharp and fancy iron upon the sky, yet chiefly to establish, rather than a flinging-upward, its intense rigidity, pride-in-ornateness, and vigor, and its opposal of the sky. [p. 48]

The interior is then shot with the same detail and rhythm, except that the surrealism creeps back: the camera "looks at itself close and hard in the mirror, beginning very softly to purr (the reduced dry sound of its motor)" (p. 49), arms reach out and turn off faucets, a clock is seen to coil its spring rigidly. However, a difference appears in this half of the film. Where before the style had tried to satisfy, then destroy logical preconceptions (nuns are holy; boy scouts are good; crucifixes inspire reverence), or to evoke absurdities by conjoining the expected and unexpected (a young man of thirty might be expected to drink a martini, but not acid; a young girl of nine might be overdeveloped, but not with a "submergedly desperate nympholeptic face"), Agee now wastes little time in creating or allowing an emotional basis for his irony. With the quickening beat of the storm, the rhythm of the film is wound up like the clock mainsprings on camera. The viewer is all too ready for the emotional release of the storm, the destruction of the ornamented house, and the restoration of the world to the innocence of the children's games.

This rich and surreal treatment of revolution accurately represents the precise point at which the intellectual and emotional atmosphere of the 1930s detonated Agee's sensibility. The failures of capitalism, the loathing of Nazism, which combined to throw many writers and intellectuals into the open arms of the Communist party, had evident force in Agee's feelings. His adaptation of *Man's Fate* also demonstrates the impact that Communism, seen as a suffering brotherhood, had on him. But, more to the point, the arbiter of "The House" is the cosmic force of the weather, and the peacemakers are children. The film shows no abused proletariat, unless it is the timid figure of Leopold Bloom, run down by hearses, driven by creatures perverse in their indulgence. Quite simply, Agee's political position, if it can be called that, was anarchistic. But the stance he usually assumed in the face of 1930s radicalism was aesthetic. "Still have my ways of believing in artforart," he wrote Macdonald from Florida on April 14, 1936, commenting on Archibald MacLeish's reception into the Communist party, "and, more specially, of conviction that Marx, Marx plus Freud for that matter, isn't the answer to everything." Later that same year, in an article entitled "Art for What's Sake," he democratically chided readers of *New Masses* for their rejection of artistic experimentation:

It should be remembered not only that for every instrument of art the world swarms with revolutionary material but that any new light on anything, if the light has integrity is a revolution.

And that if by no means all of this material is discernible through the most strictly Marxian lens, the man who is using the lens had better get his eyes seen to. [New Masses 21(December 15, 1936):48]

The metaphor of art as an instrument, specifically a lens, is significant, for it might be argued that in writing "The House," Agee had used something closer to a knife. Almost certainly Father Flye had commented on Agee's paragraph commending Huey Long's assassin. For in Agee's first lengthy letter from Florida—he told Macdonald in January he had written fairly steadily up until the first of the year—he tried to explain his impulse:

... many kinds of remarks I make, etc. are not so facilely or hatefully brought about as they may seem—that if some whole set of things becomes something of which in its details I seem pretty glibly scornful, that all the same comes out of a good deal of not so cynical effort to understand what that set of things means. I'm not claiming to be honest, because I realize that I'm not, but I do swear that I want to be and try to be: and that makes you angry against things, including yourself, which are not honest: and when (like, say Will Hays) one of them appears so to you for a long enough time, your anger and scorn become automatic. [Letters, pp. 86-87]

The words have a familiar ring. They seem to be an explanation of the state of mind Agee had described in 1932, of that scorn he felt for himself as well as for others because he feared that his efforts were being misspent. But in Florida in 1936 he has no more explanation for the reaction than a description of how it comes about. He is still beset by the confusion between the thinking and feeling self and the objects of thought and feeling. In writing "The House" Agee had set down single or collective objects of his experience—a legless pencil vendor, a nun, a rotarian, boy-scout parades, funeral processions, an old house and its artifacts—and as he closed in on them with his imagined camera, they changed shapes in front of him. Agee himself raises an appropriate point in discussing another surreal film treatment of revolution. In his 1947 review of Jean Vigo's *Zero de Conduite* (1933), he noted the film's aesthetic independence: "The boys in *Zero* are seen as they see each other" (*Reviews*, p. 264). The opposite is ture in "The House"—the characters are seen as Agee treats them. They emerge from a perspective of distant respectability to be imaginatively distorted by the artist's moral passion. In this treatment, not only is reality deceptive, but the feeling self is perilously unstable about the American present.

As a result, the best work to emerge from Agee's 1936 leave of absence concerns his past. "Whose grievance ever yet delayed the sun?" (Poems, p. 58, l. 2) he asks in "A Song," published in June in *transition*. The question implies the reconciliation he had expressed earlier in "John Carter": a contrast of the mutable and immutable, followed by a rejection of the confusing present and an acceptance of the changeless rhythms of nature and the cosmos. In a remark about his own thematic preference, Agee, in his letter from Florida, had declared to Macdonald: "What a job cd be done on the equilibrium of nature." Thus, reinforced by his own separate peace, Agee wrote a number of poems about his childhood and Knoxville. In the same letter he characterized half of them as "unfinished-experimental," the other half as "finished but lacking interest & vitality." Undoubtedly the finest piece was the prose "Knoxville: Summer of 1915," which he read to Father and Mrs. Flye at St. Andrew's on his way home to New York. But all the pieces reflect this injunction concerning his writing which Robert Fitzgerald has found in one of his notebooks:

My need for tone, tension & effect in writing limits me very badly. Yet cd. be good. But in many ways needless effort. And in many ways false. Its attempt in long run: to give, at once, frame and fluescence to pic. of universe. Seem to feel I have no right to give the looseness till is established the tightness wherein it moves. . . Must throw brain into detail. ["Memoir," p. 35]

This need for "tone, tension & effect" is most apparent in a poem such as "Lyric"—published under the title "Vertigral" in the *Saturday Review*—where effect is the net result of the poem:

Demure morning   morning margin   glows cold   flows foaled:
Fouled is flown   float float   easily earth before   demurely:

[Poems, p. 153, ll. 1-2]

In these first two lines the spacing, use of the colon, repetition, alliteration, and assonance are more apparent than the sense. Although Agee will evoke an intelligible effect, such as "morning margin   glows cold," and add to its intelligibility by these devices, his main intent is to use words as units of sound, reproducing a nonverbal "Word Music." The same criticism may be made of "In Memory of My Father (Campbell County, Tenn.)"; but that poem exhibits a certain progressive experience. It is a description and evocation of nightfall even in its opening lines.

Bluely, bluely, styles from stone chimneys crippling smoke of hickory larch and cedar wood of elm of the white oak. The quell night blues above.[7]

That these lines are reminiscent of the verse in "Knoxville: Summer of 1915," which opens with "Now is the night one blue dew" (*Death*, p. 13), is no coincidence, because both pieces grow out of similar memories: that of Rufus being put to bed, in the poem at his grandfather Agee's; in the story at his grandfather Tyler's. In fact, the similarity of metaphor, of night, of parental care, of sleep, is one of the few aids in reading the subtle symbology of "In Memory of My Father."

The experience of this poem, of night, is told as though it were happening. The words are arranged to suggest the aural tones of night in order to create a precognitive apprehension of the experience. Syntactically, then, certain words need not signify anything—though some meaning may be read into "The quell night blues above." But the words must evoke the deadening and thick ignorance of night. This effect of precognitive rather than cognitive apprehension was wrought in "Lyric," which concerned the experience of morning. But the result of that poem was precisely as Agee had noted: it gave "frame and fluescence" to a picture of the universe; but the poet had no right to this "looseness" without establishing the "tightness" upon which it moved. "Must throw brain into detail," he had adjured himself. Therefore "In Memory of My Father" mixes techniques, nonverbal evocation, verbal images, and musical variations:

The blue night blacks above. Lamps: bloom in their glasses and the stars: splinter and glister glass. Warmth: slops from the pigsty. In the barn pale hay, tussled in teeth, darkness, a blunt hoof. The black night blinds above.

This poem cannot be declared unsuccessful. Indeed, it achieves what it attempts: to evoke the sensual quality of the experience of night and of sleep, and thus to convey a profound realization that the earth's natural concern for itself is a metaphor for human love. However, the poem is at best an experiment. That is, it attempts to use words and phrases as notes and bars of music. And although the attempt is justifiable, the accomplishment is different from—and, it may be argued, less than—what words chiefly do: signify objects and their relationships.

Considering the fine accomplishments of "Sunday: Outskirts of Knoxville" and "Knoxville: Summer of 1915," these experiments in "Word Music" were not in vain. As Elizabeth Drew has written of "Sunday: Outskirts of Knoxville":

Throughout, we are kept constantly aware of the two visions which compose the poem. The idyllic vision persists within the shadow of the realistic vision until the closing prayer brackets both. This dual vision is not sustained by means of direct reference but always by means of suggestion within the visual or sound pattern.[8]

Her remarks are an appropriate introduction to the poem, which can be seen to rely on traditional devices for its musical quality:

There, in the earliest and chary spring, the dogwood flowers.

Unharnessed in the friendly sunday air
By the red brambles, on the river bluffs,
Clerks and their choices pair.

Thrive by, not near, masked all away by shrub and juniper,
The ford v eight, racing the chevrolet.

They can not trouble her:

Her breasts, helped open from the afforded lace,
Lie like a peaceful lake;
And on his mouth she breaks her gentleness:

Oh, wave them awake!

They are not of the birds. Such innocence
Brings us whole to break us only.
Theirs are not happy words.

We that are human cannot hope.
Our tenderest joys oblige us most.
No chain so cuts the bone; and sweetest silk most shrewdly
    strangles.

How this must end, that now please love were ended,
In kitchens, bedfights, silences, women's-pages,
Sickness of heart before goldlettered doors,
Stale flesh, hard collars, agony in antiseptic corridors,
Spankings, remonstrances, fishing trips, orange juice,
Policies, incapacities, a chevrolet,
Scorn of their children, kind contempt exchanged,
Recalls, tears, second honeymoons, pity,
Shouted corrections of missed syllables,
Hot water bags, gallstones, falls down stairs,
Stammerings, soft foods, confusion of personalities,
Oldfashioned christmases, suspicions of theft,
Arrangements with morticians taken care of by sons in law,
Small rooms beneath the gables of brick bungalows,
The tumbler smashed, the glance between daughter and husband,
The empty body in the lonely bed
And, in the empty concrete porch, blown ash
Grandchildren wandering the betraying sun

Now, on the winsome crumbling shelves of the horror
God show, God blind these children!

[Poems, pp. 65–66]

The song rhyme of the second stanza, the modulations in rhythm in the third ("Thrive by, not near, masked all away"), the interior rhymes in the fifth ("lace" to "lake" to "break"), the assonance, alliteration, even the irregular beat of details in the long climax, all produce a quiet and graceful music integral to the sense of the verse. It should also be noted that the construction of metaphor is exactly opposite that of "In Memory of My Father." In that poem Agee had begun in the abstract:

Tell me was ever love. so gentle in the hand. so tender in the eye. was ever love: more lovely to the loved. The secret water smiles upon herself; the blue cedar: stands in his stone of smoke.

The question is vague, assuming an attitude unknown to the reader until he encounters "The secret water smiles upon herself," which gives him a basis for understanding the later direct address: "sweet tended field now meditate your children : child, in your smokesweet quilt; joy in your dreams." Then the reader comes to realize that the earth's love for its existing self is analogous to a father and mother's love for a child. In "Sunday: Outskirts of Knoxville," however, Agee begins the metaphor in the concrete to imply the mythic:

Her breasts, helped open from the afforded lace,
Lie like a peaceful lake;
And on his mouth she breaks her gentleness:

The implied embrace of water and sky, found in the "Voyages" of Hart Crane, is one instance of Drew's emphasis: that the poem's dual vision of idyll and reality is sustained by "means of suggestion within the visual or sound pattern." However, it is the tendency toward detail, obviously encouraged by Agee's writing from the perspective of a camera in "The House" and "Man's Fate," which marks a crucial accommodation in his style.

Since leaving Harvard Agee had written poetry and journalism. His sole surviving effort at fiction is poor and unfinished.[9] The journalism, of course, is full of detail, but it is used for the most obvious of ends and fails, in his terms, any proper moral evaluation. The poetry, on the other hand, is lyrical and, finally, attempts to evoke moods or feelings which are subliminal to perception and intellection. Spliced together, however, the two elements of Agee's talent become that concise realization of music he had described in the soliloquy of "They That Sow": "the facts as they are, tempered by sternness and pity and calm." This style constitutes Agee's best writing, characteristic of "Knoxville: Summer of 1915," [10] of sections of *Let Us Now Praise Famous Men*, and of *A Death in the Family*. It is rich yet tempered prose, more suggestive of the senses of hearing and taste and touch than of sight alone; and it relies on these primary perceptions rather than on any complexity or sophistication perceived by the intellect. There is a sense of loss, but not of opportunities or of experiences, such as is felt in F. Scott Fitzgerald's or Sherwood Anderson's writings. There is a sense of drama, but not of people in conflict, such as is found in the novels of Hemingway or John Dos Passos. Agee's vision is more fundamental: the loss and drama of sensation, the primary perceptions of material transiency and of the tension which exists between the act and the shadow. Having read it, who can forget:

> *A street car raising its iron moan; stopping, belling and starting; stertorous; rousing and raising again its iron increasing moan and swimming its gold windows and straw seats on past and past and past, the bleak spark crackling and cursing above it like a small malignant spirit set to dog its tracks; the iron whine rises on rising speed; still risen, faints; halts; the faint stinging bell; rises again, still fainter; fainting, lifting, lifts, faint forgone: forgotten. Now is the night one blue dew. [Death, p. 13]*

Or

> *The nozzles were variously set but usually so there was a long sweet stream of spray, the nozzle wet in the hand, the water trickling the right forearm and the peeled-back cuff, and the water whishing out a long loose and low-curved cone, and so gentle a sound. First an insane noise of violence in the nozzle, then the still irregular sound of adjustment, then the smoothing*

into steadiness and a pitch as accurately tuned to the size and style of stream as any violin. So many qualities of sound out of one hose: so many choral differences out of those several hoses that were in earshot. Out of any one hose, the almost dead silence of the release, and the short still arch of the separate big drops, silent as a held breath, and the only noise the flattering noise on leaves and the slapped grass at the fall of each big drop. That, and the intense hiss with the intense stream; that, and that same intensity not growing less but growing more quiet and delicate with the turn of the nozzle, up to that extreme tender whisper when the water was just a wide bell of film. [Death, p. 12]

Prose such as this does not defy analysis; it merely makes it obsolete. Enough has been written of its constituents and of its various intentions. It will be sufficient to mention that this achievement happened very seldom in Agee's work, often in the wake of periods of great pressure, when he forgot what he knew and wanted of writing and performed innocently. Such innocence is apparent in the closing lines of both "Sunday: Outskirts of Knoxville" and "Knoxville: Summer of 1915." Having led his reader through a field of variegated sensations, he has created that sense of mystery at the end of these two pieces which properly gives rise to prayer. He had explained this effect in his own way to Dwight Macdonald, who perhaps had thought the closing line—"but will not, oh, will not, not now, not ever; but will not ever tell me who I am"—(*Death*, p. 14) too obvious. "The effort," Agee wrote him in 1938 "was to make something equivalent to playing a plain c-major scale at the end of a less plain piece of work,—and to be best set up without defense or stage direction." Ultimately, this is the way he should have had it every time, but he did not.

After a three-week stay with Father and Mrs. Flye at St. Andrew's, the Agees returned to New York in the first week of May 1936. Jim was no longer working formally for *Fortune,* but he had agreed to take articles from time to time when he needed the money. He therefore began to rewrite and type the work he had written in Florida until one day, several weeks after his return. Robert Fitzgerald has described the event.

> . . . *Jim appeared in my office unusually tall and quiet and swallowing with excitement (did I have a moment?) to tell me something in confidence. It appeared very likely, though not yet dead sure, that they were going to let him go out on a story, a story of tenant farming in the deep South, and even that they would let him have as his photographer the only one in the world really fit for the job: Walker Evans. It was pretty well beyond anything he had hoped for from* Fortune. *He was stunned, exalted, scared clean through, and felt like impregnating every woman on the fifty-second floor. So we went over to a bar on Third Avenue.* ["Memoir," p. 15]

The assignment was actually very similar in nature and scope to the work Agee had done on the Tennessee Valley Authority. He was to describe the daily and yearly life of an Alabama sharecropper family, analyze the economics of Southern farming, and comment on the contributions of individual Southern liberals, local unions, and state and federal governments. Quite generally, this kind of article reflected an earlier compromise between the editor-in-chief, Henry Luce, and the young New Dealers on his staff. Dwight Macdonald, who was working for *Fortune* until shortly before Agee's return, notes sarcastically that "Luce was divided between his pro-business convictions and his journalistic instinct, which told him the CIO was news and that the wonders of American Cyanimid Co weren't." [1] Despite his initial enthusiasm, however, Agee grew skeptical, not only of his ability but, as he told Father Flye, "more of *Fortune's* ultimate willingness to use it" (*Letters*, p. 92). His attitude probably had less to do with his own rebelliousness than with the times. Several of Agee's friends, Macdonald among them, had recently resigned from *Fortune*. A backlash to the magazine's "leftward trend" was making itself known among subscribers. Moreover, upon returning from Alabama, Agee realized the truth of his suspicions: "The trip was very hard, and certainly one of the best things I've ever had happen to me," he wrote Father Flye; then he added, "Writing what we found is a different matter. Impossible in any form and length *Fortune* can use" (*Letters*, p. 94).

The date was September 8, 1936. *Let Us Now Praise Famous Men* was not to be published for five years. In the interim Agee saw three publishers, dissolved two marriages, scraped out some kind of living, borrowing from friends, doing some writing for *Fortune,* writing little else because creative work depended on his moods, finally giving up to review books for *Time* in October 1939, while on the periphery of vision Western Europe was disintegrating beneath the boots of Hitler's Wehrmacht: Spain, Czechoslovakia, Poland, France. By the time *Famous Men* emerged from the presses of the Houghton Mifflin Company in September 1941, whatever commercial design had given it birth—to show the crippling and incredible rural poverty, unearthed and popularized in the mid-1930s because the urban middle and upper classes who read were themselves broke and liked learning of others worse off than themselves—by 1941, that was forgotten, or at least not salable. The book was remaindered, and Agee went on to write movie reviews, for which he is justly remembered. Nevertheless, there was the book—"A book only by necessity," Agee wrote; "a piece of the body torn out by the roots might be more to the point" (*FM*, pp. xvi, 13). There were the weeks with the tenant families in the summer of 1936. In the midst of all the world's pain and suffering, of Agee's lack of work, lack of desire, lack of conviction, there had been his single attempt to describe the "whole nature and problem of existence."

Let Us Now Praise Famous Men is dominated by two themes:
individual compassion and the common need of the human family. These are represented by epigraphs from Lear's soliloquy on
the heath and from the Communist *Manifesto*. The entire volume
is divided into two books, Evans's photographs and Agee's writing. Agee's book is composed of prefatory material and three
parts, interspersed by three essays entitled "On the Porch," concerning aesthetic problems. The prefatory material consists of
three sketches of Evan's and Agee's attempt to contact tenant
farmers. Part One is a series of prose poems on the human family.
Part Two gives statistical reports of the tenants' money, shelter,
clothing, education, and work. Part Three is a narrative of Agee's
first night with the tenant Gudger, his initiation into the subject
as it involves his compassion and recognition of the common need
of the human family. Appropriately, this part is entitled "Inductions."

But, more pointedly, *Famous Men* is the attempt to describe a
situation and two individuals' response to that situation. The situation was that "moment" Agee had spoken of in "They That
Sow," or a "juncture of space, time and consciousness" in which

All the length of the body and all its parts and functions were
participating, and were being realized and rewarded, inseparable
from the mind, identical with it: and all, everything, that the
mind touched, was actuality, and all, everything, that the mind
touched turned immediately, yet without in the least losing the
quality of its total individuality, into joy and truth, or rather,
revealed of its self, truth, which in its very nature was joy, which
must be the end of art, of investigation, and of all anyhow human
existence. [FM, p. 225]

Or, more specifically, knowing the exact proportions of Gudger's
house.

It is, having examined scientifically or as if by blueprint how
such a house is made from the ground up, in every strictly sized
part of its wood, and in every tightening nail, and with nearly
every inch of this open to the eye as it is within one of these
rooms, to let all these things, each in its place, and all in their

*relationships and in their full substances*be at once, *driven upon your consciousness, one center. [FM, p. 184]*

The similarity between this impression and Agee's indications of how to photograph the old Victorian mansion in "The House" is striking. Essentially the link is in his way of seeing reality. Often he implies a comparison between his eye and that of a camera, clearly an influence of the similarity he saw between film form and the graphic quality of the works of Blake and of Joyce. But behind this technique is his fundamental respect for reality, his incarnate belief that everything that is is holy. For instance, in the preface to *Famous Men* he notes his intention "to recognize the stature of a portion of unimagined existence," to inquire "into certain normal predicaments of human divinity."

The immediate instruments are two: the motionless camera, and the printed word. The governing instrument—which is also one of the centers of the subject—is individual, anti-authoritative human consciousness. [p. xiv]

Taken together, these phrases set down a desired relationship between the subject and the object of cognition. Existence has a "stature" of "divinity," "normal" to it and "unimagined." The purpose of the book is to record that truth with minimal transformation by means of a camera and "anti-authoritative human consciousness." As Samuel Hynes has pointed out, *Famous Men* "is above all a book about *knowing,* about how one human being may realize the existence of another, and of the obstacles to such knowledge." [2]

On the other hand, it is necessary to recognize the one peculiar bias which is the major obstacle to Agee's knowing the human beings he has encountered. The predominant literary influence in *Let Us Now Praise Famous Men* is James Joyce. Agee's qualified statement that "everything the mind touched turned immediately . . . into joy and truth, or rather, revealed, of its self, truth, which in its very nature was joy" places him very close to the spirit of the closing couplet of Keats's "Ode on a Grecian Urn" and to the Thomistic concept of *claritas,* which Stephen

Dedalus explicates toward the end of *A Portrait of the Artist as a Young Man.*[3] Furthermore, Agee's statement is a deliberate turning away from the Romanticism found in the poetic theories of Wordsworth and Coleridge and central to the poetry of Walt Whitman and Hart Crane, among others. For he is saying that it is not the mind's perception or shaping of a thing which makes it truthful, but rather the perception of the thing's truth which makes the mind joyful. Hence Agee is forced to conceive of the unlikely possibility of a purely objective percipient. Although he is adamant in his assertion of "individual and anti-authoritative," or of "unassisted and weaponless consciousness" (*FM*, p.11)—as if the words themselves could wipe away preconceptions—he is constantly at war with his own effort. One of the mildest, yet most revealing examples of this confusion occurs when he writes:

For in the immediate world, everything is to be discerned, for him who can discern it, and centrally and simply, without either dissection into science, or digestion into art, but with the whole of consciousness, seeking to perceive it as it stands . . . and all of consciousness is shifted from the imagined, the revisive, to the effort to perceive simply the cruel radiance of what is. [FM, p. 11]

In restating Stephen Dedalus' aesthetic of the "radiance" of common objects, Agee has added that the perception of reality is painful or "cruel," recalling his own vulnerability to people and experiences. Undoubtedly his appreciation for the camera, especially the purist work of Walker Evans and Mathew Brady, as well as his conception of an "unassisted and weaponless consciousness," form an attempt to temper the conflict between his own emotional susceptibility with the tenants and their lives and his desire to see them clearly for what they are. Unless he could control his own sympathies, he ran the risk of producing something as patronizing as Erskine Caldwell's and Margaret Bourke-White's 1937 photojournalistic study of sharecroppers, *You Have Seen Their Faces* or Dorothea Lange's and Paul Schuster Taylor's 1939 work in the same genre, *An American Exodus.*[4] But Agee's reasons for control were hardly dictated by professional or personal vanity. He was, as Robert Fitzgerald has emphasized, looking for the truth and a way of seeing it; and most importantly, he was looking at the South, at people who bore more than a passing resemblance to his own ancestors and whose simple efforts at keeping themselves alive seemed to him both tragic and courageous.

Joyce's influence, then was natural to Agee for two reasons: Joyce's work demonstrated the kind of control Agee yearned to have over his material; and Joyce's life was a total commitment to his art. According to Fitzgerald, Agee had told a friend in 1935 that Joyce had so thoroughly gotten into his blood that he had to "master and get over that influence if he were ever to do anything of his own" ("Memoir," p. 3). However, Joyce's influence in *Famous Men* was indeed in Agee's blood rather than on his mind. There was little left for him to get over. Joyce's work was an answer to his concerns about aesthetic distance, but it affected Agee in such a way that the writing of *Famous Men* may be described as an almost unconscious paradigm of the process Stephen Dedalus describes in *Portrait* to define an epic. "The simplest epical form," Stephen says, "is seen . . . when the artist prolongs and broods upon himself as the centre of an epical event and this form progresses till the centre of emotional gravity is equidistant from the artist himself and from others" (*Portrait*, pp. 214-15). The same process of balancing his emotions between the tenant Gudger and himself, between the source and the place of his response, was outlined by Agee in a forceful passage:

> *I am confident of being able to get at a certain form of the truth about him,* only if *I am as faithful as possible to Gudger as I know him, to Gudger as, in his actual flesh and life (but there again always in my mind's and memory's eye) he is. But of course it will be only a relative truth.*
>
> *Name me one truth within human range that is not relative and I will feel a shade more apologetic of that.*
>
> *For that reason and for others, I would do just as badly to simplify or eliminate myself from this picture as to simplify or*

invent character, places or atmospheres. A chain of truths did
actually weave itself and run through: it is their texture that I
want to represent, not betray, nor pretty up into art. [FM, pp.
239-40]

In writing *Famous Men,* therefore, Agee realized that his ability
to maintain this "centre"—to shift the balance from the self to a
projection of the self in its relation to the event—was crucial.
Joyce had accomplished the task in *Ulysses* by the deceptively
simple device of a mythic narrative and a well-disguised persona.
But such choices were not open to Agee. He was not writing
fiction, nor was his narrative overtly mythic, and his persona,
though a projection, was hardly disguised.

This last point was most obvious to the critics in 1941. *Time's*
reviewer, as well as C. Wright Mills writing five years later, saw
Agee's persona as an "intrusion," a "stylistic pratfall." Trying to
be witty, *Commonweal's* John C. Cort spoke with inadvertent
understanding: "the author . . . is in much more tragic condition
than any exploited sharecropper." However, at least two reviewers understood the persona's significance. Ruth Lechlitner,
writing for the New York *Herald Tribune's* Book Review guessed
that "as readers of this book we have moved in on Mr. Agee. . . .
Perhaps this, whether intentional or not, is the book's chief social
documentary value." Selden Rodman, however, went to the heart
of the matter:

Part of the greatness and unique quality of "Let Us Now Praise
Famous Men," then, is its structural failure, its overall failure as
the "work of art" it does not aim or presume to be and which
from moment to moment it is. Were it written straight, *proceed-*
ing logically without these savage asides from the arrival of its
"spies" (Agee and Evans) through their initiation and undoing
and departure, it would be dishonest. The unparalleled intensity
of much of the writing, the extra-ordinarily nightmarish and yet
sacred sense of the whole—*the feeling that this is the tragedy of*
most of the two billion inhabitants of the planet extended back-
ward and forward in space and time—the communication of

Christian (most anti-Churchly) brotherly love, the extreme rever-
ance for man and nature—none of these would be remotely pos-
sible coming from a "sophisticated," "sensitive," "confused,"
"upper-class," "American," "writer" in the year 1941 without an
accompaniment of the most profound guilt. And it is because this
guilt is shamelessly exposed in its most raw and unattractive
shape, that "Let Us Now Praise Famous Men" will be spat
upon—and years hence (unless the country is given over to the
fascists or the faith-healers of "far away" democracy) read.

As Rodman perceived, Agee's epic depended upon what he eu-
phemistically called the book's "structural failure," and the heart
of that failure was Agee's deeply and actually involved persona.[5]

Both truths, the record as well as the response, made up *the*
truth. Agee's method was dictated, like any artist's, not by an
evasion, but by a total commitment to his own experience; and it
is in such a "moment" or "situation" that the Alabama trip provides for him, that his poetic tangents and experiments as well as
his journalistic background anneal under the cooling pressure of a
personal response to certain human beings. The mixture of various perspectives in "The House," or even in "Sunday: Outskirts
of Knoxville," might suggest the progress Agee had made toward
his epic persona. In each case they follow the lines laid down by
Dedalus in the *Portrait:* that the lyric is "the simplest verbal
vesture of an instant of emotion" and that the epic can be "seen
emerging out of lyrical literature" (*Portrait*, pp. 213–14). However, a clearer indication can be found in one of Agee's poems,
"Lyrics," published in the *Partisan Review* in the Winter 1937
issue (pp. 40–43) written toward the end of his stay in Florida.
Although the title indicates a number of separate verses, each
stanza is related to the others in much the same way as one of
W. H. Auden's song groupings. Furthermore, the poet's perspective evolves throughout the poem in a way which bears a significant relationship to the persona of *Famous Men.*

1

Remember limber thunder in the deaf : the metal
tasting air:

Cities like silly medals lay : wind:
Flashed the whole forest pale:

Spasm and blindness blenched and the bunched cloud
5   *Delivered his blue columns.*

Remembering thunder: deliberating in the shadow
   cold: the fuse air:

   The paltry metals on that pitiful breast: the wind
   Violating the pale forest crest:

   Twittering blaze, the bunched cloud
10   *Voided, and slept aloof, the miles*
   Restored into the sun, the clean sun
      Sheened in his scope:

Remembering unlimbering thunder in the deafness
and the tinder air:

   The pinned and pendant cities: in the woods
15   *A whole year's generations struck one white:*

Collaborative, and determinate thunder:

2

Soft heaven shuts: at length the latest
Plaintiff is silenced and the ample south
Absorbs him unlamenting:

20   *Here, moreover, subdued, the seed*
Meditates and shall publish the usual flower:

And he, restored, bouncing on bloodied twig,
Schemes out his spiritual music.

3

His subtle throat is broken on the air;
25   *(Reproachfulness, outbreast the wind)*
That pointed eye, narrow hands, the fluted bone
   Lie with the forest fall.

Yet with the year, shall, with the wrinkling leaves,
The frail shell break, the fragile monster breathe, and,
30   Falling, wing find air: and talk to god
      Much like his grandfather in his time.

4

Tonight sweet heart I think in graves of the wild earth
      forgotten,
Straws of old harvest whom the sun ignores,
Bones, and their bran, congratulate.

35   I do not think they pity us.
They pity less than they are glad.

All that was ardent and which now is air:
Warms round our wrestling here.

5

Heal, hardy air, harm in earth.
40   And yield these lungs the while to breathe
It takes to whisper out that worth
Whose cloudy forehead you enwreathe.

6

Not for your ease or pleasing was the air
Mild, the while past, and loving with the earth.
45   What for the seethe of health up breadth of summer
I cannot guess, but doubtless not for us.

Cruellest and dingiest of the squatters we
Who wring and craft and these this field apart.
From the huge kindness of their kingdom's edge
50   The citizens peer seldom but to hide.

However, there are harms about the heart
We never dealt us, but can only serve.
Serve them then as we must, to further harm,
And help what can; and meantime let who will

55 *Lift on this glimmered dark his joy, his small surmise,*
    while,
Serious and unregarding, with stiff hands the heavens
    Rust and unwreathe the world.

7

Squared behind intellectual hedges:
Bloodhounds and rifles arranged to guard:
60 *Be sure: subtly, how cheated faith avenges.*

Make the mind only a little too hard:
Suspect too fearfully the irrational:
Your feet will break through tunnels under your
    yard.
You will be unseated by an unforeseen international.

65 *Have you surely added it up to the right amount?*
Shall florid history never split your pot?
Have you taken the animals thoroughly into account?
Are you sure it is still yourself you dream of or not.

8

Your end's to end forever
70   *War's wrath, the rotted laws.*
But man in his last anger
    Shall kill for larger cause.

9

Tears are the touchers of that secret earth
No alien rains attend; be therefore tears;
75 *Grieve, and your holy land accords you mirth;*
Pity brings wrens of the most batflight fears.

10 A Nursery Rhyme.

Glimmer, glimmer, universe
Whom storms of mysteries immerse:
Nebulae not grieved for Zion
80 *The blown seeds of a dandelion:*

How I wonder by what rules
Beyond the touch of local fools
In the anarchic spring unborn
85 *Whose front lawn you shall adorn.*

What immeasurable child
Shall your burning have beguiled
Before another picks you dry
And puffs your promise down the sky.

In what city shall that be
90 *And in what strange vicinity.*
(Hark my friend we've had our day,
School is out, they're on their way.)

Gods snub each other on our back stairs
The ancient time contemned as snares.
95 *Our galaxy, so runs the hope,*
Is mirror for a telescope.

Curved brightness is a beveled jewel
Examining minute renewal.
All things undreamt, one atom's core.
100 *One spark of sand, its endless shore.*

There thrive fish the dark sea down
Unsuspicious of our town.
We each are lumps in a same leaven
And Friday's print amazes heaven.

11 Education of the Prince.

105 *He must strike down his father's cedar shadow:*
Sever his mother's terrible and sorrowing mouth;
Abandon, under their stone labels in the charted
    meadow
His tired friends, and start the journey south.

Follow the man on the hill with the fire on his back:
110 *Outbrave the monstrous lady of the woods:*

Speak dialects, snap twigs deceptively, destroy his
name:
He must make the dark journey under the hollow sea.

The most important aspect of this lyric sequence is the gradual yet evolving shift of the points of view. In effect the poem becomes a self-sustaining conversation. Although the first word, "Remember," seems addressed to the reader, the repetition of the participial form in line 6 makes it clear that the poet is addressing himself and that the storm he is remembering is, through repetition, becoming an object of meditation. With the first words of the second section, "Soft heaven shuts," the poet begins a narrative point of view. The "Plaintiff" who is silenced is presumably the thunder, but the "seed" nourished by the storm to "publish the usual flower" obviously implies the poet and his poem. In the third section the poet speaks objectively of himself in a way that lets him move to the subjectivity of the fourth section with ease. From then on he switches point of view freely, at the same time moving his perspective from himself to his "sweet heart," to the "graves" of his ancestors, the "harms about the heart," and finally to the "universe." Although he is speaking from the subjective point of view of the fourth section, the fifth section is a prayer, the sixth, seventh, and eighth are a warning or prophecy, the ninth is narrative, the tenth is prayer, and the eleventh is a combination of narrative and prophecy.

Two metaphors loosely integrate the shifting focuses of Agee's evolving persona: the blossoming seed and the air. The air is not only the physical atmosphere, but also the medium of the poet's voice and his and his lover's and his ancestor's desires.[6] In the first section, the air carries the thunder, whose "metal" taste, "fuse," and "tinder" qualities suggest the canons and bombs of the Spanish Civil War. In the third section, it carries the poet's voice, in the fourth the ardor of his ancestors. Its use is especially interesting in light of a comment to Father Flye written toward the end of Agee's stay in Florida:

The weather: wonderful now, and there have been days and

evenings of a kind I've never seen the like of elsewhere: like
honey if latter were breathable and weren't sticky. [Letters, p.
90]

This remark recalls the first line of the fifth section, "Heal, hardy
air, harm in earth," and the pessimism of the first quatrain in the
sixth, presumably addressed to his wife, Via. Finally, it is the air
in the tenth section which carries the "blown seeds of a dandelion" throughout the universe, uniting the two metaphors and
completing the evolution of the persona.

The "seed" of the second section, figuratively the poet, is now
a full-blown flower, an object of wonder to himself. Hence the
actualized persona, symbolized by the flower, stands outside his
figurative potential, the "blown seeds of a dandelion." The coupling of metaphors and symbols provides a context for the images
of the nursery rhyme which couple microcosm and macrocosm:

Our galaxy, so runs the hope
Is mirror for a telescope.

and,

All things undreamt, one atom's core.
One spark of sand, its endless shore.

However, the first ten sections of the poem, cyclic in their evolution of the poet's perspective, are also prelude to the final stanza,
"The Education of the Prince." This title, as well as the last line
of the tenth section, only vaguely suggests an identity. "Friday's
print" which "amazes heaven" seems an awkward reference to
Christ. Another prince who had to "strike down his father's cedar
shadow," "sever his mother's terrible and sorrowing mouth," and
"abandon . . . His tired friends" was Hamlet. Perhaps Agee means
to suggest both Christ and Hamlet in this final lyric, but the most
obvious prince, no prince at all, is himself.

The significance of "The Education of the Prince" and the
ultimate significance of "Lyrics" is in many ways similar to
Agee's dedicatory verse in *Famous Men*, "(To Walker Evans." Its
opening stanza is directly addressed to his photographer friend:

Against time and the damages of the brain
Sharpen and calibrate. Not yet in full,
Yet in some arbitrated part
Order the façade of the listless summer.

Since the first word of the second stanza is in the plural, however,
it must refer to both Evans and himself:

Spies, moving delicately among the enemy,
The younger sons, the fools,
Set somewhat aside the dialects and the stained skins of feigned
    madness.
Ambiguously signal, baffle, the eluded sentinel.

Having identified a common concern and disguise, Agee shifts his
emphasis to the concerns of "The Education of the Prince":

Edgar, weeping for pity, to the shelf of that sick bluff,
Bring your blind father, and describe a little;
Behold him, part wakened, fallen among field flowers shallow
But undisclosed, withdraw.

Not yet that naked hour when armed,
Disguise flung flat, squarely we challenge the fiend.
Still, comrade, the running of beasts and the ruining heaven
Still captive the old wild king.

                                                    [FM, p. 5]

It is clear that both "The Education of the Prince" and "(To
Walker Evans" are concerned with the mystery of the relationship
between a father and son, symbolized by the son's obligation to
rescue the significance of the father. Both poems, moreover, are
couched in the language of subterfuge, so common to W. H.
Auden's poetry at the time. The son in this verse is Edgar, son of
the Duke of Gloucester in *King Lear*. Disguised as a fool, he is
commanded by his blind father to take him to the edge of a bluff
so that Gloucester can commit suicide; instead, Edgar brings his
father short of the edge, describes the precipice, and watches him
jump into the flowers of the field. More relevant to the techniques of *Let Us Now Praise Famous Men*, however, Agee demon-

strates in "Lyrics" and "(To Walker Evans" his ability to shift his "centre of emotional gravity" from a lyrical self meditating on its own experience to an epic projection of the self in relation to others.

The process by which he accomplishes this shift from a lyric to an epic voice can be compared to atomic fission, when particles bombard a center which then explodes and bombards other centers. If Agee's consciousness is conceived as the original atom, then the various "planes" from which he records his subject can be compared to the exploding particles. The description of his subject matter in a notebook illustrates a similar bombardment:

> *At the centre, every recapturable instant of those eight weeks spent in the middle south.*
> *Everything that led up to those eight weeks.*
> *Everything that has proceeded from or will proceed from them.*
> *Every relevant problem or issue which is raised by this material.*
> *At the centre again: our selves, and our instruments. These secondary instruments are the still camera and the printed word. The primary instrument is individual human consciousness.*
> *Again at the centre: these three families, chosen with such pain to "represent" their kind; with whom, for a little while, we intimately lived, and whom we watched.*
> *Then immediate environment; and, insofar as we have perceived it, the general south.*[7]

Here the entire subject is divided into juxtaposed "centres" of atmospheres, authors, and tenants. The bombardment which impinges on all is reminiscent of the motion of the sense data of the Gudger house being driven upon Agee's own consciousness, "one center."

One aspect of his effort is to verify that "a chain of truths did actually weave itself and run through," that objects of his sensation did provoke responses of anguish and joy—"this at least illusion of personal wholeness or integrity" (FM, p. 227). But the most important aspect of the book is Agee's attempt to write of his experience without imagining it. This led him to conceive of the tenants in the same terms he conceived of himself: "how am I to speak of you?" he asks. "Let me say, then, how I would wish this account might be constructed:

I might suggest, its structure should be globular: or should be eighteen or twenty intersected spheres, the interlockings of bubbles on the face of a stream; one of these globes is each of you.

The hear, nerve, center of each of these, is an individual human life. [FM, pp. 100, 101]

Because he did not invent narrative nor disguise himself, his effort to give the book epic balance involves simply a representation of the conflicts or responses of his own conscious experience. His task is not only to perceive or to recall perceptions, but also to record them as they were recalled, as well as to acknowledge the peculiar biases which control the process. *Famous Men,* then, becomes not merely a report of the reflective self, but also a transcription of the processes of reflection: on the self, on the objects of its experience, and on its own report.

Throughout the book, but especially in discussing its aesthetics, Agee undoubtedly confuses his reader. In explaining the necessary selection involved in recording, for instance, he cites Joyce's effort in *Ulysses:* "It took a great artist seven years to record nineteen hours and to wring them anywhere near dry." But then, he argues, selection does not obscure the significance of an experience, since he believes that "the universe can be seen in a grain of sand." Backtracking quickly to avoid the mysticism of Blake's image, Agee adds, "I am again not trying any such job here. On too many other counts I simply do not think the experience was important enough to justify any such effort." But since he cannot deny his tendency to universalize the experience, he records in a footnote, "I am no longer sure of this." Then, in exasperation, he adds, "all I want to do is tell this as exactly and clearly as I can and get the damned thing done with"; but he is again forced to footnote: "This is more complicated now." Finally he sums up his own as well as the reader's feeling:

The whole job may well seem messy to you. But a part of my

*point is that experience offers itself in richness and variety and in
many more terms than one and that it may therefore be wise to
record it no less variously. Much of the time I shall want to tell of
particulars very simply, in their own terms; but from any set of
particulars it is possible and perhaps useful to generalize. In any
case I am the sort of person who generalizes: and if for your
convenience and mind I left that out, I would be faking and
artifacting right from the start. [FM, pp. 242-45]*

Thus, while Agee adheres to Dedalus's Thomistic epistemology to
the effect that reality reveals its truth to the perceiver, he is
forced to acknowledge the inevitable failure of the epic process—
in shifting the center of his emotion from reflection to relation,
there is the tendency to generalize and the danger to distort. But
there is no other way, he argues. His life differs from the lines of
the tenants only in its particulars:

*. . . for this human sphere is all one such interlocked and mar-
velously variegated and prehensile a disease and madness, what
man in ten million shall dare to presume he is cleansed of it or
more so than another, shall dare better than most hesitantly to
venture, that one form of this ruin is more than a millionth
preferable to another? [FM, p. 108]*

ii

The writing and the form of *Let Us Now Praise Famous Men* is
an attempt to represent the "richness and variety" of Agee's total
consciousness of his experience, from the time he received the
assignment to the moment when he read the galley sheets. The
method by which he objectifies his consciousness is to record his
experience from four "planes" of attention:[8]

*That of recall; of reception, contemplation, in medias res. . . .
'As it happened.' . . .
By recall and memory from the present. . . .
As I try to write it. . . . [p. 243]*

The first plane, Agee tells the reader, is used in the three sections entitled "On the Porch." The writing is essentially meditative, the point of view is after the fact, remembering, analyzing, and recording sensations of remembrance. The second plane, " 'as it happened,' " is described by Agee as "the straight narrative at the prow as from the first to last day it cut unknown water" (p. 243). Ideally the point of view should be in the first person and the present tense; however, except for particular places within other planes, Agee uses the first-person, present-tense narrative consistently in only one section—"The Gudger House," in the part labeled "Shelter." He explains how narrative is usually subsumed under the third plane, "by recall and memory from the present":

It seems likely at this stage that the truest way to treat a piece of the past is as such: as if it were no longer the present. In other words, the 'truest' thing about the experience is now neither that it was from hour to hour thus and so; nor is it my fairly accurate 'memory' of how it was from hour to hour in chronological progression; but is rather as it turns up in recall, in no such order, casting its lights and associations forward and backward upon the then past and the then future, across that expanse of experience. [pp. 243–44]

Not only are these remarks a blueprint for the book as a whole, in that sections are arranged without regard to chronological order, but they also indicate the mixture of perspectives found within any one section. For example, in "Inductions," a section of " 'as it happened'," Agee interrupts to say: "If I were going to use these lives of yours for 'Art,' if I were going to dab at them here, cut them short here . . . I would just now for instance be very careful of Anticlimax" (p. 366). The interruption is, of course, a "problem of recording" but uttered within the direct narrative point of view and intended to be overheard by the reader. Again, Agee's angry chapter, "Education," which is written as "recall and memory from the present," is of such a biased, though persuasive, point of view that it ultimately becomes a "problem of recording."

Above all, the perspectives are not merely documentary. "Trying," Agee argues, "to represent, to reproduce, a certain city street, under the conviction that nothing is as important . . . . you try to give the street *in its own terms*":

You hold then strictly to materials, forms, colors, bulks, textures, space relations, shapes of light and shade, peculiarities, specializations, of architecture and of lettering, noises of motors and brakes and shoes, odors of exhausts: all this gathers time and weightiness which the street does not of itself have: it sags with this length and weight: and what have you in the end but a somewhat overblown passage from a naturalistic novel: which in important ways is at the opposite pole from your intentions, from what you have seen, from the fact itself. [pp. 235–36]

"The fact itself," Agee would have the reader understand, is not only a representation of things in their own terms, but more importantly, a representation of them in terms of the response they effect within the perceiver. "You share," he writes, repeating his summary from the soliloquy of "They That Sow," "the naturalist's regard for the 'real,' but have this regard for it on a plane which in your mind brings it level in value at least to music and poetry, which in turn you value as highly as anything on earth" (p. 238).

This controlling bias or "regard for the real" was based on the belief that reality itself creates beauty. "I would insist," he writes in *Famous Men*, "that everything in Nature, every most casual thing, has an inevitability and perfection which art as such can only approach" (p. 233). And it is, he explains, "one reason I so deeply care for the camera" (p. 234). So closely resembling Joyce's concept of epiphany, these ideas were later expanded in the rough and published drafts of an essay introducing Helen Levitt's collection of photographs of Spanish Harlem, written sometime in the 1940s. In the essay's opening paragraph Agee defines two kinds of still photography: static and lyric. Any photographer's task, he writes, is

to perceive the aesthetic reality within the actual world, and to

make an undisturbed and faithful record of the instant in which
this movement of creativeness achieves its most expressive crystal-
ization.[9]

Static photography, of which Walker Evans' and Mathew Brady's
work are examples, "is generally the richest in meditativeness, in
mentality, in attentiveness to the wonder of materials and of
objects." Lyric photography, of which Levitt's work is an example, "is richest in emotion" and "most nearly related to the
elastic, casual, and subjective way in which we ordinarily look
around us" (p. 5). Using lyric photography as his example, he
explains in the rough drafts what he had meant by "the aesthetic
reality within the actual world":

In Helen Levitt's photographs of New York and Mexico City,
the moment is usually so fleeting that what we see is, instead, like
the turning of light along the side of a fish as he moves in the
water.
   The water in this case, is the world of actuality—that is, the
world we see with our eyes. The flashing of the fish is that mo-
ment in which the actual world creates its own kind of aesthetic
reality.[10]

Although Agee admitted that "in every other art which draws
directly on the actual world, the actual is transformed by the
artist's creative intelligence into a new and different kind of reality" (*A Way of Seeing*, p. 5), this sensual nuance, the variance of
sense data arrested in space and time by the lens of a camera, is at
the heart of his way of seeing or what he calls a "regard for [the
real] on a plane which . . . brings it level in value at least to music
and poetry." Such a lyrical moment of joy explains the "dignity
of actuality" and Agee's attempt to cope with it by the arrangement of language in such a way as to capture every shade and
nuance. The simple impingement of light upon a sensitive surface
within a camera caught and reported "the instant in which this
movement of creativeness achieves its most expressive crystaliza-
tion." But as a writer, Agee was obligated, not only to perceive
and to record this simple but exact impingement of light, but also

to report all its further journeys in the recall of his consciousness. The record of these moments of epiphany is of the essence of Agee's accomplishment in *Famous Men,* for it incorporates the thing seen in its moment to moment variance as well as the mind's changing relationship to and residual effect from it.

Perhaps the finest example of this kind of writing is found in a passage of "Shelter" entitled "In The Front Bedroom: The Signal." Because it is illustrative of the core of Agee's way of seeing—his word-by-word, sentence-by-sentence effort as well as overall concern for form in the work—the passage must be quoted and analyzed at length.

I lie where I lay this dawn.)

If I were not here; and I am alien; a bodyless eye; this would never have existence in human perception.

It has none. I do not make myself welcome here. My whole flesh; my whole being; is withdrawn upon nothingness. Not even so much am I here as, last night, in the dialogue of those two creatures of darkness. What is taking place here, and it happens daily in this silence, is intimately transacted between this home and eternal space; and consciousness has no residence in nor pertinence to it save only that, privileged by stealth to behold, we fear this legend: withdraw; bow down; nor dare the pride to seek to decipher it:

At this certain time of late morning, then, in the full breadth of summer, here in this dark and shuttered room, through a knothole near the sharp crest of the roof, a signal or designation is made each day in silence and unheeded. A long bright rod of light takes to its end, on the left side of the mantel, one of the small vases of milky and opalescent glass; in such a way, through its throat, and touching nothing else, that from within its self this tholed phial glows its whole shape on the obscurity, a sober grail, or divinity local to this home; and no one watches it, this archaic form, and alabastrine pearl, and captured paring of the phosphor moon, in what inhuman piety and silent fear it shows; and after a half minute it is faded and is changed, and is only a vase with

light on it, companion of a never-lighted twin, and they stand in
wide balance on the narrow shelf; and now the light has entirely
left it, and oblates its roundness on the keen thumbprint of pine
wall beside it, and this, slowly, slides, in the torsion of the en-
gined firmament, while the round rind of the planet runs in its
modulations like a sea, and along faint Oregon like jackstrewn
matches, the roosters startling flame from one another, the dark-
ness is lifted, a steel shade from a storefront.

Here also, his noise a long drawn nerve behind him, the violin
wasp returns to his house in the angle of the roof, is silent a half
minute, and streams out again beneath eaves upon broad light.

But he: he is not unwelcome here: he is a builder; a tenant. He
does not notice; he is no reader of signs. [FM, pp. 187–88]

The first paragraph establishes a very complex set of verbal
relationships. The entire section, "Shelter," under which "The
Gudger House" is a subsection, is written " 'as it happened.' "
Thus the verb of the first sentence is in the present tense, but the
adverbial clause identifies the subject more closely with the *place*
of "(On the Porch:1," "where I lay this dawn," and the *event* of
"(On the Porch:3," "the dialogue of those two creatures of darkness." This exchange between two wild animals had already taken
place the night before, but it has not yet taken place in the book.
With the first sentence, then, there is a dissonance of perspectives;
the author sees four events: the dawn, the signal, the bedding
down of "(On the Porch:2" and "(On the Porch:3," and the
dialogue of the animals, which he places in the past, present, and
future of the reader. The author's persona knows of the four
events, all of which have occurred during his past night's stay on
the porch. But the reader has experienced only two events—the
dawn and the signal, that which *is* taking place and that which *has*
taken place. He knows of the two other events—the dialogue of
the animals and the bedding down—only because he is now told
that they have taken place, but he has no clue to their arrangement in fact or in the book. To him, they are like missing notes
of musical counterpoint, reiterated in "(On the Porch:2" and
"(On the Porch:3."

This arrangement of planes and calculated omission of detail is a concrete illustration of what Agee means when he states that *Famous Men* is "loosely, an experiment in sonata form."[11] The sonata itself is a three-movement composition scored for one or two instruments. It works off variances of two and three. For example, the first movement of Beethoven's *Pathétique* piano sonata has two themes which are restated three times; the same is true of its second and third movements. There are, however, variations of key, notes and tempi within both major and minor themes. Moreover, the "sonata form" is a generic term for the outline of a movement, usually the first, of a symphony. *Famous Men*, with its two books having two themes, three parts, and three codas, could be seen as either a sonata complete in itself or the first movement of a larger work. Certainly this view corresponds to Agee's stated intention for the volume: "the beginning of a larger piece of work; and to stand of itself, independent of any such further work as may be done" (*FM*, p. xiv). The three perspectives of the passage from "Shelter"—that of the author, the persona, and the reader—are analogous to the centers of consciousness mentioned in Agee's notebook and can also be seen to figure in the larger form as any three-note entity in the statement of a major musical theme.

Another aspect of the first paragraph is a conflict of planes. True enough, the paragraph and what follows is written on the plane of " 'as it happened.' " But with the identification of the place of "On the Porch" enters the plane of attention dealing with that place: "reception, contemplation, *in medias res*." "If I were not here," begins the contemplation. The depersonalization of the narrator, "a bodyless eye"—recalling Emerson's "transparent eyeball"—is an insistence on the purely observable. But the dialogue between the planes of the observable and the contemplative is a groundswell between the "scientific" and the "artistic," which will result in the passage's overall tone and poetry.

The object of observation, the passage of a slant of light into and out of the throat of a glass vase on the Gudger mantel, is an "aesthetic reality" created by the actual world. Agee reads it as a "signal or designation," a marking or consecration that takes place daily between the vase, the home, and the globe. From precise observation of fact ("through a knothole near the sharp crest of the roof . . . a long bright rod of light") evolves a sexual metaphor ("takes to its end . . . one of the small vases of milky and opalescent glass") and a religious metaphor ("a sober grail, or divinity local to this home"). The progress of the paragraph, with its distinct punctuation and prepositional ligatures, its exploding metaphors and consistency of thought, its intentional dissymmetries and meditative composition, is clearly baroque in ancestry. [12] Its intention is not only to report, but also to characterize and to represent the process of characterization.

To record the "dignity of actuality," then, depended not only on recording what was seen, but also on representing the process by which it had been seen, by which it had been recalled, and by which it was reported. To have taken the record further—to have made this joyful response to actuality a catalyst in the making of an invention—would have been to make "art." But in order to do so, Agee would have had to violate the essence of his perception—that which *had happened* in the "marvelously variegated" way in which it had happened. Clearly, at times Agee does dismiss the process, so overwhelmed is he by his joy that it becomes catalytic, as he describes in the opening of "A Country Letter":

I feel that if I can by utter quietness succeed in not disturbing this silence, in not so much as touching this plane of water, I can tell you anything within realm of God, whatsoever it may be, that I wish to tell you, and that what so ever it may be, you will not be able to help but understand it. [p. 51]

But he explains this element of his writing in "(On the Porch:2":

Though I may frequently try to make use of art devices and may, at other times, being at least in part an 'artist,' be incapable of avoiding their use, I am in this piece of work illimitably more interested in life than in art. [p. 242]

For most readers these are undoubtedly the most troublesome

lines in Agee's book, and they have led to a number of superficial readings of his intentions. Primarily there has been a complete disregard of his admonition: " 'Above all else: in God's name don't think of it as Art" (p. 15). What Agee means by "art" is what most Romantics have meant by that term since the publication of the "Preface to the Second Edition" of the *Lyrical Ballads:* a "spontaneous overflow of powerful feelings" or the projection of joy or anguish into invented figures. Agee had conceded that what he was trying to do in *Famous Men* (record his joy and anguish in relation to real people) could possible be an art, but not one which involved, as Romantic art did, the suspension of disbelief. His intention, he maintained, was antithetical to Coleridge's, because he could no longer accept the possibility of an organic concept of language.

Agee's ideas on language so influenced by I. A. Richards, his own journalism, and his poetic experiments, demand some discussion. His comments bear a striking resemblance to Emerson's. F. O. Matthiessen has written that "no American writer before Emerson had devoted such searching attention to his medium." [13] And certainly no writer after Emerson has done so much as Agee. The similarities between them can be deceptive, however. To put it very simply, Agee might have wished he were Emerson; he would have enjoyed the ability to believe, as Emerson put it in his essay "Nature," "Words are signs of natural facts." [14] For Agee writes in *Famous Men:* "The cleansing and rectification of language, the breakdown of the identification of word and object, is very important" (p. 237); and he writes Father Flye at this time that there should be a law "which interdicted the use of all words to which the reader cannot give a referrent" (*Letters,* p. 104). But there was no such law nor cleansing and rectification, and Agee wrote *Famous Men* with this truth in mind. Words, he was forced to conclude, "are the most inevitably inaccurate of all mediums of record and communication" (p. 236). His list of "other anglosaxon monosyllables" in the final pages of the book is intended as an implicit proof of this statement. Perhaps it can be argued that Agee's poetry and fiction are more respectful of Emerson's remaining propositions—"Particular natural facts are symbols of particular spiritual facts" and "Nature is the symbol of spirit"—but it should be pointed out that Agee is careful in *Famous Men* to distinguish between fact and fiction:

In a novel, a house or person has his meaning, his existence entirely through the writer. Here, a house or a person has only the most limited of his meaning through me: his true meaning is much huger. [p. 12]

Later, commencing a formal discussion of language, he declares: "Words cannot embody; they can only describe," and again he pursues the distinction:

. . . a certain kind of artist, whom we will distinguish from others as a poet rather than a prose writer, despises this fact about words or his medium, and continually brings words as near as he can to an illusion of embodiment. [But such] art accepts the most dangerous and impossible of bargains and makes the best of it, becoming, as a result, both nearer the truth and farther from it than those things which, like science and scientific art, merely describe, and those things which, like human beings and their creations and the entire state of nature, merely are, the truth. [p. 238]

Ultimately in writing *Famous Men* Agee did not wish to accept that "most dangerous and impossible of bargains," to speak Emerson's or Whitman's ideal world into being. No doubt he could not deny that words named objects and that from time to time, in lyrical sections of his book, he wrote "art." But words also have many other functions which a student of I. A. Richards, conscious of their "full body," could not overlook. Thus he attempts, for instance, to describe the objects found on Gudger's mantel.

A small round cardboard box:
(on its front:)

> *Cashmere Bouquet Face Powder*
> *Light Rachel*

(on its back:)

The Aristrocrat of Face Powders
Same quality as 50c size.

Inside the box, a small puff. The bottom of the box and the bottom face of the puff carry a light dust of fragrant softly tinted powder. [p. 172]

This is not, as he noted of Whitman's poetry, "a category of beloved objects." [15] The adherence to sense data is actually closer to Joyce's writing in *Ulysses*, for the words are descriptive, rather than being simply things that are spoken. "It is much simpler than that," Agee insists.

It is simply an effort to use words in such a way that they will tell as much as I want to and can make them tell of a thing which happened and which, of course, you have no other way of knowing. [FM, p. 246]

The suspicion arises that in these seemingly endless and tortured discussions of aesthetics Agee is protesting too much. Certainly his description of the shaft of light touching the vase on the Gudger mantel; his reminiscence of Emerson in the words, "I am a bodyless eye"; the metaphorical shape of the passage; his admission to being a "reader of signs," which causes him to feel guilty and to find it difficult to look the Gudgers in the eye— these seem to be "art" of the very kind he is rejecting. But there is a crucial difference, abetted in part by Agee's contemporary consciousness. Many of his reasons for rejecting his own impulses and needs to make "art" are based on the complex understanding of his language, which he acquired from the beginning of his poetic experimentations in the early 1930s through the writing of *Famous Men.* Agee no longer hoped to create the organic literary diction he had described to Father Flye some few months before he attended I. A. Richards' Harvard lectures. Not only had this teacher made the possibility of such a diction suspect, but the periodicals for which Agee worked made a mockery of language every day. America of 1936, America of 1941, he declared, had had enough of the "Rube Goldberg articulation of frauds, com-

98

A Way of
Seeing

promises, artful dodges and tenth removes" (*FM*, p. 236) per-petrated by contemporary usage. Therefore, Agee's mere declara-tion that his writing originated in experience, and not in the mind, did not do half as much to remove him from the tradition of Emerson and the Romantics and place him beside Joyce and the moderns as did these tortured discussions of the limitations of his own medium. Moreover, his attention to photography and the clean-lensed manner in which it duplicates Dedalus' description of cognition seemed more respectful of reality than of the inherent urge he had to shape it to his own design.

iii

What remains is postscript, the education of the prince. There must be acknowledgment of the fact that *Famous Men* is not only a book by James Agee but also a book about James Agee—"a co-vert autobiography," as his friend W. M. Frohock has called it. [16] This fact was overlooked by two astute commentators, Dwight Macdonald and Lionel Trilling. [17] Both felt that the characters of the tenants did not come alive. Comparing the book to *Moby-Dick*, Macdonald wrote:

> *Melville's people are "bigger than life," they have will, conscious-ness and passion, they struggle and act, but the Ricketts and the Gudgers and the Woods, as presented by Agee, are passive, beaten, without much will or consciousness, victims of life with no more ambitious aim than to keep going from day to day.... Melville had the creative force to give his theme a dramatic form; Agee's book is a series of notes from which such a drama might be worked up but which is not fused into a whole.*

Trilling found the book not a literary failure, but

> *... a failure of moral realism. It lies in Agee's inability to see these people as anything but good. Not that he falsifies what is apparent: for example he can note with perfect directness their hatred of Negroes; and not that he is ever pious or sentimental,*

like Steinbeck and Hemingway. But he writes of his people as if there were no human unregenerateness in them, no flicker of malice or meanness, no darkness or wildness of feeling, only a sure and simple virtue, the growth, we must suppose, of their hard, unlovely poverty. He shuts out, that is, what it is a part of the moral job to take in. What creates this falsification is guilt—the observer's guilt at his own relative freedom.

Both critics miss the point in a very important way. Agee is not writing fiction but fact; his emphasis is on the mystery, not the evocation, of what is. For instance, in telling the story of Annie Mae's sister Emma, Agee does "note with perfect directness" a vast network of jealousy and lust and pride and fear which constitutes the situation. But there is no way he can evoke it without imagining it, unless he confesses to some of the same sins himself. And insofar as he had no part in the situation except as an onlooker, there is no other appropriate emotion than "guilt at his own relative freedom." In part, it is his classic dichotomy: art uses reality, and in the case of the tenants, the reality is their "exclusive property" and the "privilege of the people at the bottom of that world" (*FM*, p. 203). But in a larger sense this dissonance between himself and the tenants, which provokes his guilt, is the whole mystery of his undertaking. He suggests some of its causes in his notes on "Beauty" following the section "Shelter." But nowhere does he express it so eloquently as in an excised portion of the manuscript dealing with "Work":

That I was not born a tenant farmer's son is no doing of mine: nor is it any doing of mine that I was born as I happened to be, among relative advantages. But every human advantage is a theft; and the worst of it is, that by this theft by which one gains, another is deprived; and that the one who is deprived is the one who has earned what he is deprived of by hard and hopeless work, or is his children who must suffer for him. I feel intense guilt towards every such man and woman and child alive; and I suggest you need to feel it too; and that that sense of guilt cannot possibly be enough, nor the wish to expiate sufficient.

It is in the terms of this intensely felt guilt that I wish I could
write of a tenant's work: in such a way as to break your back
with it and your heart if I could: but still more: in such a way
that 'innocent' of them though you are, you might go insane with
shame and with guilt that you are who you are, and that you are
not what some one of these persons is, who is living, while you
are living. Good God if I could only make even this guilt *what it*
is: not just some piece of pathology or of metaphysics, but the
literal thing it is, the literal earth. That because you are as you
are, they are as they are: living persons, each with as sacred a
claim upon all existence as your own: and that of this existence,
they get what they get of it, and are made what they are made,
and you get and are made what you are. [18]

This is not the pious expression of "mea culpa" of a New Deal
liberal. It is the recognition of a mystery permitting of no solution, either by New Deal reforms or by the Communist party's
goal to destroy capitalism. It is a mystery, partly of chance and
partly of design, but nonetheless a mystery, the perception of
which, Agee believed, should fill the heart with humility and
gratitude and care.

In essence Agee's journey in *Let Us Now Praise Famous Men* is
an initiation into this mystery. The prefatory sections of the
book are vignettes: of a businessman asking a landowner to show
him his tenants' houses; of an unexpectedly ashamed journalist
who has indirectly caused a landowner to force his Negro tenants
to interrupt their midday meal to sing for him; of a stranger
asking directions from a diffident sharecropper family, a humili-
ated but well-bred Easterner who is mauled by the cropper's
cretin child; of an awkward and eager writer-on-assignment who
frightens a Negro couple by running up behind them to ask an
insignificant question. The following section, Part One, "A
Country Letter," is pervaded by another false front, a sense of
paternalism, of entering the tenants' sleep and their dreams, of
interpreting their lives, of presuming that Emma's misfortune can
be restored by his lovemaking. These disguises are propped up by
concern and its accompanying sin, superiority. Part Two, "Some

Findings and Comments," is for the most part a clenched-teeth appraisal of the tenants' lives, their money and how it is earned, their shelter and of what it is made, their clothing, their education and its deceits, and their work. But the closing section of the book rips off the disguises and even the moral outrage. Appropriately, it is entitled "Inductions," for it is a new beginning. Here Agee tells of his first encounter with the tenants, of his and Evans' repulsion for everything rural and of their retreat to Birmingham, finally of Agee's meeting with George Gudger and his family, the occasion of a summer rainfall which brings about Agee's need for Gudger's food, companionship, shelter, and help. Combined with his nausea at eating Annie Mae Gudger's cooking is the simple joy that the Gudgers are giving the food to him and that he is receiving it from them. He has learned to "feel what wretches feel," not to imagine how they feel. He has learned to share their pain yet to be fed, to be bitten by their bedbugs yet to sleep. Thus Agee's final posture suggests that the way to love one's fellowman is not to do anything for him; that would be moral presumption. Rather, love exists as a state of acceptance based upon the recognition of common human needs. Ultimately these needs specify themselves in the expressions of the individual, in his language, his clothing, his house, his way of work and life. But to truly discover another's needs, taking all exigencies into account, is to discover one's own.

The education of the prince, then, is complex. It partakes of the learned values of the tenant experience as well as of Agee's Southern background. Harvard and Exeter, *Fortune* and Greenwich Village, were not merely veneer to him. By chance, they were integral. And insofar as they betrayed his sense of himself as the son of a rural Tennessee pioneer family, they were paradoxically destructive. In the Gudger kitchen Agee recognizes this relationship in an anguished moment of self-discovery.

> ... *the feeling increased itself upon me that at the end of a wandering and seeking, so long it had begun before I was born, I had apprehended and now sat at rest in my own home, between*

two who were my brother and my sister, yet less that than some-
thing else; these, the wife my age exactly, the husband four years
older, seemed not other than my own parents, in whose patience
I was so different, so diverged, so strange as I was; and all that
surrounded me, that silently strove in through my senses and
stretched me full, was familiar and dear to me as nothing else on
earth, and as if well known in a deep past and long years lost; so
that I could wish that all my chance life was in truth the betrayal,
the curable delusion, that it seemed, and that this was my right
home, right earth, right blood, to which I would never have true
right. For half my blood is just this; and half my right of speech;
and by bland chance alone is my life so softened and sophisti-
cated in the years of my defenselessness, and I am robbed of a
royalty I can not only never claim, but never properly much
desire or regret. And so in this quiet introit, and in all the time we
have stayed in this house, and in all we have sought, and in each
detail of it, there is so keen, sad, and precious a nostalgia as I can
scarcely otherwise know; a knowledge of brief truancy into the
sources of my life, whereto I have no rightful access, having paid
no price beyond love and sorrow. [FM, p. 415]

The nostalgia he finds is not only a sad remembrance, but also a
selection of details from his past of which his present life seems
to him a betrayal. His nostalgia is a "truancy into the sources of
[his] life," his father's rural Tennessee blood. However, he has
"paid no price" for this nostalgia. He is not a tenant, nor will he
ever approach reality with the tenant's primitive needs and instincts. Agee's perception is a paradox, for while he feels at home,
he has no right to claim it as such: he has betrayed that ancestry
which he can "never properly much desire or regret." Thus it
might be himself he is allegorizing in his concluding section, "(On
the Porch:3," in the description of the two animals calling to
each other in the darkness. The tentative probing of their cries
seems to approximate Agee's attempt to reach his own past. As
well, it could be a description of the relationship between Agee
and the tenants or Agee and his readers:

. . . at all times it was beyond even the illusion of full apprehension, and was noble, frightening and distinguished: a work of great, private and unambitious art which was irrelevant to audience. [FM, p. 466]

Like the cry of his nostalgia, the cry of the animals is based on their common loneliness. But above all, the cry is consumed far more by wonder than by torment.

Agee could hope that *Let Us Now Praise Famous Men* would be "a work of great, private and unambitious art which was irrelevant to audience." But what remained with him upon its publication was a sense of its inadequacy. "A sinful book," he wrote Father Flye, "at least in all degrees of 'falling short of the mark' " (*Letters*, p. 131). Yet in another sense Agee had recognized the potential for a new aesthetic. In notes accompanying a revision of the "Preamble" he had jotted down some ideas for a series of periodicals similar to those he had submitted in October 1937 with his Guggenheim application and had worked on for at least two or three years with Robert Fitzgerald.

> *An exposition of methods by which corruption betrays itself.*
> *A sampling of letters.*
> *A sampling of news and magazine clips.*
> *Series: poems: composed of advertisements, news photographs, and photographs personally made. . . .*
> *A record & analysis of one week's work on Time. . .*
> *An attack on the M of M Art.*
> *On motion pictures as caught midway in becoming respectable.* [19]

Two parts of this series, Agee's essays on photography accompanying the works of Helen Levitt and of Walker Evans, were eventually published in a conventional format. [20] The format Agee had originally conceived came very close to what he had seen as the ideal for *Famous Men:*

> *If I could do it, I'd do no writing at all here. It would be photographs; the rest would be fragments of cloth, bits of cotton,*

lumps of earth, records of speech, pieces of wood and iron, phials of odors, plates of food and of excrement. [FM, p. 13]

In one respect it is ironic that this minimal transformational art has appeared only very recently in contemporary graphic exhibitions. Agee was in part engaged in adapting its precursor to literature in an aesthetic, practised by Cocteau and Picasso among others, that held the subject of a painting to be the excuse for the artistic process. In another respect, because the book brings so many approaches to bear on a single subject, it is very simply a masterpiece. What to Agee and his readers was a confusion between his desire for an organic poetic diction and a hypersensitivity to the ambiguities of language was actually a demand for a new way of seeing, where all objects, including language, had simple integrity and truth and where the artist's task, rather than finding form or giving shape to imagined things, was to arrange or produce that which already existed. Undoubtedly, because of this accomplishment, *Famous Men* is different from any work of its time. Yet the book is also a characteristic American work of genius in that it is more relevant to its future than to its present or past. As Agee said of it, it was "merely portent and fragment, experiment, dissonant prologue" (*FM*, p. xv).

The two years preceding the publication of *Let Us Now Praise Famous Men* were possibly the most difficult of Agee's life. Harper & Brothers was trying to sign him to a contract, including the stipulation that "certain words be deleted which are illegal in Massachusetts" (*FM*, p. xiv). After an unpleasant correspondence with this publisher, the manuscript was released in the fall of 1939. At that time the Agees were living from hand to mouth, and in October Jim finally took a job with *Time*, reviewing books for $45 a week. After the first of the year—about the time of the birth of his son, Joel, in March—he separated from his wife Alma and began seeing Mia Fritsch, whom he later married. From then on events began to approach equilibrium. Houghton Mifflin accepted the book in the spring of 1941, and it was published in the fall. In October he left the "Books" department and took over *Time's* movie reviews. Mia Agee has remarked that "he found book reviewing terribly hard, because he couldn't develop a quick knack at judging a book. He was delighted when they changed him to movies."[1] A year later, in the fall of 1942, Margaret Marshall asked him to write a longer film column for *The Nation*. Into these reviews, shortened for *Time,* he poured his energy during and after the Second World War. As Robert Fitzgerald has written, at last he had "found the kind of journalism answering to his passion" ("Memoir," p. 59).

It was no accident, then, that in those obscurely anxious days of late 1939 and early 1940 Agee had begun to reread Joyce. As he was to write in a February review of Herbert Gorman's biography, Joyce's life was "almost a Bible of what a great artist, an ultimately honest man is, and is up against."[2] His "heroism" was "a complete self-faithfulness"; and how far Agee felt he was from that kind of commitment he expressed in a letter to Fitzgerald in December, 1940:

*I am thirty-one now, and I can conceivably forgive myself my
last ten years only by a devotion to work in the next ten which I
suspect I'll be incapable of. I am much too vulnerable to human
relationships, particularly sexual or in any case heterosexual, and
much too deeply wrought-upon by them and in turn much too
dependent in my work on "feeling" as against "intellect." In
short I'm easily upset and when upset, incapable of decent work;
incapable of it also when I'm not upset enough. ["Memoir," p.
52]*

It is easy to imagine from this excerpt the kind of model and
ideal Joyce could be for Agee. During this time especially—in
which he was frightfully close to compromising his ambition to
be a serious writer and which was typically beset with insomnia,
promiscuity, and an almost suicidal devotion to other people's
problems—Agee used any subject as an excuse to deepen his belief
in his writing. Politics, he told Father Flye in March, only had the
effect of driving him "towards art, psychology and religion" (*Letters*, p. 125). And in an earlier letter, written in August 1939,
when he had begun to reread *Portrait*, he made these comments
in connection with the movie, *Goodbye, Mr. Chips*:

*. . . something of what it is talking of I consider to be sacred
territory. In proportion to sacredness of territory one needs to be
merciless of mishandling (no matter how sincere) and merciless
towards the sincerely part-good which can almost always be moving and inspire generosity towards its weakness. In certain respects this mercilessness in non- or anti-Christian. It is absolutely
required however of a "good artist," meaning a "pure" "heart,"
meaning a "moral" "man."* [Letters, pp. 118–19]

Undoubtedly there was a connection between his reaction to
Joyce's *Portrait* and to *Mr. Chips* as well as to the event looming
on the horizon, his return to the Luce organization. And there is
little need to note that Agee's conclusion to this apologia describes his typical ambivalence, a call to Joycean "mercilessness,"
which is at its core "moral."

According to the evidence of his notebooks, about the time

Agee was writing Father Flye this letter he was also jotting down ideas for the introduction to *Famous Men*. The conjunction of the writing with his reading of *Portrait* apparently made him realize how indebted he was to Joyce for the aesthetics of his book. For he told Father Flye that *Portrait* made him

> . . . *ashamed ever to have thought I'd read it before, and exceedingly suspicious on the whole question of when or how or how soon to read what: unless there is certain to be rereading; and suspicious even then; and suspicious for that matter of my illusion that I am reading it now. I would suspect a chemical rule on reading as in 'influence,' 'imitation,' and 'plagiarism'; that in reading or being influenced 'successfully' one does as much work as the authors did originally.* [Letters, p. 117]

Perhaps Agee was mindful of the influence of Walker Evans' photographs on the writing of his book—what he would note shortly thereafter in reference to Helen Levitt's work, that "the actual world creates its own kind of aesthetic reality," his echo of Dedalus' description of the moment of an epiphany, when a thing's "soul, its whatness leaps to us from the vestment of appearance."[3] Whatever specific relationship he had in mind, the dependence of *Famous Men* on Joyce's epiphany is apparent not only in an examination of that book, but also in Agee's continued references to the relationship between words and images throughout his film criticism. For instance, in an October 1946 review of *The Raider*, Agee wrote of its use of documentary material, "that without rhetoric or comment it became automatically poetic." And he added what might be termed a cinematic theory of the racial unconscious:

> *all that is necessarily fictional is anchored as short as can be managed to what is known to have been so* [Reviews, p. 224]

Likewise, in reviewing John Huston's documentary *San Pietro* a year earlier, he wrote:

> *Somewhere close to the essence of the power of moving pictures is the fact that they can give you things to look at, clear of*

urging or comment, and so ordered that they are radiant with illimitable suggestions of meaning and mystery. [Reviews, p. 164]

The "radiance" Agee mentions is the same epiphanic radiance Stephen had said emanates from "the soul of the commonest object" (*Stephen Hero*, p. 213); and the sequence of radiant images "so ordered" is simply Agee's application of Joyce's use of language to cinema.

In *Famous Men* Agee had spoken of a "language of 'reality' " which would have "and impart the deftness, keenness, immediacy, speed and subtlety of the 'reality' it tries to reproduce." He went on to say, "I know of no one with this particular training or interest who is using words," but in an oblique reference to Joyce, he concluded, "though one man, at least, is doing even more difficult and more valuable things" (p. 236). The relationship between Agee's theory of photography—a theory of cognition applicable to both words and images—and Joyce's use of language is consistent and striking. It is best illustrated by Hugh Kenner's penetrating analysis of Joyce's language, where he notes that for Joyce the function of the writer is that of "setting existent beings in apprehensible (not explicable) relationships, [where] various levels of meaning are various perspectives on the richness inhering in poetic order."[4] If each word or image is manifest reality, then ordering words to form sentences or images to form sequences is to speak the "language of 'reality.' " In this language, words or images do not modify one another; rather, each word or image is an "existent being," giving rise to innumerable "levels of meaning" by juxtaposition.

Agee's expression of this principle is found as early as his "Plans for Work, October, 1937," which he submitted with his Guggenheim application of that year. He spoke of a "new movie short," where "by time-condensation, each image (like each word in poetry) must have more than common intensity and related tension" (*Prose*, p. 159–60). This analogy between word and image is mentioned also in notes for another project, the "musical uses of sensation or emotion," where a love relationship is to be presented in such a way that it is

> ... complex yet as rigid as that of mirrors set in a triangle, faces inward and interreflecting. These interreflections, as the mirrors shift, are analogous to the structures of contrapuntal music.
> Most uses would be more subtle and less describable. Statements of moral and physical sprained equations. This would be one form of poetry. [Prose, p. 159]

Essentially, then, Agee's theory of images is the same as Joyce's use of language. Correspondingly, his film criticism is especially sensitive to individual elements composing the whole. On film, each gesture, expression, movement, and setting is for Agee "radiant with illimitable suggestions of meaning and mystery."

This sensibility is clearly at work in his 1947 review of Andre Malraux's Spanish Civil War film, *Man's Hope*, where he speaks of the epiphanic mode as an "excess of energy":

> By excess of energy I mean his interest—which he may have learned from Eisenstein—in letting things and movements into his frame which have nothing to do with the central action or which enhance it only queerly and surprisingly—a guerrilla's sudden skipping change in step and his sudden hand to his sweating neck; or a dog wandering from one corner of a street scene while a ball maunders in from another—little things which brilliantly lock men and their efforts and feelings into exact real place and time of day. [Reviews, p. 240]

This fascination with the photographic record of "little things which brilliantly lock men and their efforts and feelings into exact real place and time of day" poses a question implicit in the preceding discussion. Throughout, his statements suggest a preference for a language of images rather than of words. Why then did he not simply lay down his pen and pick up a camera? The answer, of course, is not so simple. He *did* pick up a camera, in 1945 when he helped Helen Levitt and Janice Loeb film their documentary *In the Streets*. But primarily Agee was a writer. As he had once expressed to Father Flye the desire to *"write symphonies,"* it may be supposed he also wanted to *write movies*. His use of words was obviously and profoundly affected by contemporary graphic arts, especially cinema, and also, he did not possess either Joyce's patience with or knowledge of semantics. When he had planned as a student at Harvard to make a movie with a friend, his task was to be directorial. As he has described it in his April 24th, 1929 letter to Macdonald, he was to "devise shots, angles, camera work, etc.—and stories"; the friend was to "take care of the photography and lighting." This project can be compared to Agee's later work as a script writer, for it points up that he had always considered that his basic conceptions were verbal and not graphic. On the other hand, Agee's reluctance to adopt the camera as his medium is also probably related to his earliest aversion to "realism". One of the most significant aspects of his film criticism is his growing disenchantment with the value of photographic realism, specifically as he found it in war documentaries. By 1947, when Agee commented on Roberto Rosselini's *Open City*, he mentioned that the kind of film he looked forward to was not the strict documentary "but works of pure fiction, played against, and into, and in collaboration with unrehearsed and uninvented reality" (*Reviews*, p. 237). Ironically, it was this penchant for fiction, his desire not only to retain the essence of an experience, but also the freedom to shape it however he could, that resulted in his continued commitment to the medium of language.

In reviewing films Agee's critical standard was, by and large, either his experience or his imagined idea of a subject. For instance, reviewing films that touched upon his Alabama experience—John Ford's *The Grapes of Wrath*, Clarence Brown's *The Human Comedy*, Jean Renoir's *The Southerner*—Agee expresses concern for "little things"—an actor's posture, speech, facial structure.[5] But in his fiercely dedicated eulogy for D. W. Griffith,

112
Epiphany and Dream

he reveals another, more basic comprehensive, perspective of his
critical method:

*I have had several clear mental images of that war, from almost
as early as I can remember, and I didn't have the luck to see* The
Birth of a Nation *until I was in my early twenties: but when I saw
that charge, it was merely the clarification, and corroboration, of
one of those visions, and took its place among them immediately
without seeming to be of a different kind of order. It is the
perfection that I know of, of the tragic glory that is possible, or
used to be possible, in war; or in war as the best in the spirit
imagines or remembers it.* [Reviews, pp. 313–14]

Written in 1948, the terms of this review reveal essential premises
of Agee's criticism. When he speaks of *The Birth of a Nation* as a
"clarification, and corroboration" of his "mental images" of the
Civil War, Agee suggests the influence of memory and emotion on
his eye. What is more, he specifies exactly how he imagines a
filmed epiphany to take place: an impression of images in their
proper order *clarifies* his images of the Civil War; at the same time
they *corroborate* emotional values he has always associated with
those images, leading him to reaffirm his basic belief in a "tragic
glory that is possible, or used to be possible, in war."

This last phrase is particularly important in assessing Agee's
reaction to Second World War documentaries. In a review comparing the 1943 army orientation film *The Battle of Britain* with
Samuel Goldwyn's *The North Star,* Agee begins with the following observation:

*We suffer—we vaguely realize—a unique and constantly inten-
sifying schizophrenia which threatens no other nation involved in
this war. Geography is the core of the disease. Those Americans
who are doing the fighting are doing it in parts of the world
which seem irrelevant to them; those who are not, remain un-
touched, virginal, prenatal.* [Reviews, p. 55]

In the course of this review he asserts that home-front viewers have "to make up the difference as well as [they can] at second hand." Hence the function of the war documentary, as Agee sees it, is to relate Americans for whom war is immediate experience to those for whom it is only a "sense of unutterable dislocation, dereliction, absence of contact, trust, wholeness, and reference." Behind his remarks, however, Agee is presuming that a photographic record of American soldiers can *clarify* the American public's "sense of dislocation" at the same time that it can *corroborate* their desires for "trust, wholeness, and reference." For it was on the basis of these presumptions that he attacks Goldwyn's film for the "hopeless mistrust in which Hollywood holds its public" and conversely praises *The Battle of Britain* for coming "about simply enough: everyone on and off screen and in the audience, clearly trusts and respects himself and others" (*Reviews*, pp. 55, 56, 57, 58). In a word, Agee presumes that the war documentary can function as a "language of 'reality' " because he also presumes that his own belief in the "tragic glory" of war (a trust and respect combatants, even enemies, hold for one another) is shared by the participant or actor, the cameraman or film maker, and the observer or audience.

By early 1945 Agee began to see that his values were not universally held, and he expressed his dismay in this moral *caveat* to his readers:

I am beginning to believe that, for all that may be said in favor of our seeing these terrible records of war, we have no business seeing this sort of experience except through our presence and participation . . . . If at an incurable distance from participation, hopelessly incapable of reactions adequate to the event, we watch men killing each other, we may be quite as profoundly degrading ourselves and, in the process, betraying and separating ourselves the farther from those we are trying to identify ourselves with; none the less because we tell ourselves sincerely that we sit in comfort and watch carnage in order to nurture our patriotism, our conscience, our understanding, and our sympathies. [Reviews, p. 152]

Agee's change in attitude concerning the documentary is crucial, because it indicates not only a vacillation in his belief in a cinematic "language of 'reality,' " but also a doubt as to the morality implicit in his culture.[6] A key to his hesitation is found in his later parenthetical reference to the "tragic glory that . . . *used to be possible,* in war." Acknowledging, in 1943, the dangers of "second-hand knowledge," Agee had begun his film criticism believing that a treatment which respected the integrity of photographed objects could clarify and corroborate the values of those who watched. The documentary, he had believed, could bring the home-front viewer closer than anything else to a sense of the truth of war and hence allow him to make informed and sensitive choices in regard to it. But the success of the documentary was dependent upon the viewer's and film maker's sharing a common belief in the decency of humankind. Agee, it seems, assumed that everyone could share his perception, watching *The Battle of Britain,* that they lived in "a decently ventilated and healthful world, where, if only for the duration, human beings are worthy of themselves and of each other" (*Reviews,* p. 58).

1945 changed all that. Horrifying evidence indicated that the Second World War was anything but an imaginary reflection of the War Between the States, a tragic difference contested by men of honor and respect. Rather, 1945 was the year in which Agee described one half of a population "[sitting] in comfort and [watching] carnage," supposing it essential to their "patriotism," "conscience," "understanding," and "sympathy," while the other half was quite ruthlessly killing and being killed. The fear he had expressed in his original defense of the documentary, that "our great majority will emerge from the war almost as if it had never taken place" (*Reviews,* p. 55), was materializing with a subtle urgency. Within weeks of his reappraisal of the documentary, he was writing Father Flye indicating the necessity for

a detailed topical analysis of the very swift and sinister decline and perversion of all that might be meant by individualism, a sense of evil, a sense of tragedy, a sense of moral vigilance or discrimination; the perversion of virtually all nominal rationalism to the most irrational sort of uses and ends; the fear of the so-called irrational, the mock-revival of mock-religion; and well, etc. etc. Whatever dignified thing may ever have been meant by "liberalism," such a thing as a true "liberal" hardly exists any more, one no longer knows one's friends from one's enemies. I lately heard several highly intelligent people talk about the courtroom mobbing of Caretta in a way which was an exact parallel of the condoning of a lynching. [Letters, p. 138]

By March 1945 Agee, like many Americans, had lost an innocence he would never reclaim. He could no longer think of the world as "decently ventilated and healthful." Rather, it was a place where "one no longer knows one's friends from one's enemies." Only in the immediate, he indicated, were there "reactions adequate to the event." Removed by distance, informed only by flickering images, oppressed by the endless headline horrors, he could only reflect the sterile confusion of those days. Writing the lead article for *Time's* "National Affairs" section for November 5, 1945, he titled the piece "Democratic Vistas" and assembled a collage of postwar stories. He juxtaposed the homiest of anecdotes on returning veterans with the irrational and brutal. Pervading the peace, he sensed, was the urgency with which Americans wanted to forget the war and "the unkeepable secret" of the Atom Bomb and to reenter their dreamlike lives unscathed by reality. His conclusion was more than standard editorial rhetoric. It was, in a very real sense, the preface to a new era:

If civilization, or time itself in the provincial, planetary sense, was to last more than another few decades, the responsibility rested chiefly on the American people. But for wholly understandable, nonetheless tragic reasons, the American people were not very responsible toward any major responsibility. If this troubled season was any indication, they would be too busy trying to buy that wholly unpurchasable dream. ["The Nation," Time 46:24]

James Agee was always sensitive to two worlds—the present, his
sense perceptions; and the past, his values. One function his art
served was to relate them. As he had written in "They That
Sow," his art concerned "some aspects of the mind's reaction to
experience." Hence an analysis of his writing and ideas on art
must consider not only what he conceived reality to be and how
he sought to express it, but also how he reacted to it. The schizophrenia he had sensed in the national mood through the last two
years of the war was in many ways a reflection of his own mind.
During that time he vacillated between the extremes of immediate perceptions, where there were "reactions adequate to the
event," and of the values of memory, past experiences, and emotions. Initially, as he had spoken of it, the function of a cinematic
"language of 'reality' " was to clarify the total consciousness—
present and past experiences—and to corroborate the values derived from them. In his eyes the film could serve the same purpose as his own art, to relate the mind's perceptions to the mind's
reactions. But when personal values were inconsonant with what
was perceived, or when, as was true for most popular films he
reviewed, a film maker's values differed from Agee's expectations,
there was no shared premise, no common decency, upon which to
base a clarification and corroboration. Increasingly his feelings
about the end of the war, reinforced by Hiroshima and Nagasaki,
centered on the discrepancy between the values he had believed
were prevalent, or at least tacitly assumed, in American culture
and the phenomena of life around him. For this reason Charlie
Chaplin's 1947 film *Monsieur Verdoux* had a profound impact on
him, describing, as it did, a man who married and murdered women in order to support a beloved crippled wife and son. In this
film Agee perceived the metaphor of a society which forces men
to do evil in order to retain such traditional values as marriage
and home. In rough drafts for his monumental three-part review
of the picture for *The Nation* he describes the moral root-

lessness of Verdoux's life as it is symbolized in his various "homes"—the ones in which he murders wealthy heiresses and the one in which his real wife and son live. Adopting the personal pronoun, he states that Verdoux's real home

is not even really home any longer, but only a dream, a rigid dream. You carry the dream with you where you go, and on occasion you can step inside it, but then you too become a part of the dream.[7]

Not until 1947, then, was Agee able to describe the new conception of consciousness which had been growing in his thoughts since the middle of the war. Throughout this period he had been trying—in his reaction to war documentaries and his analysis of a national schizophrenia—to assess the influence of values and emotion on perception, cognition, and choice. In commenting on David Selznick's 1944 melodrama, *Since You Went Away*, Agee had described the process: "When the consciousness blurs into love, it means a fidelity to dream" (*Reviews*, p. 107). He had also, however, criticized entire productions as "dreams." For instance, in a 1943 review Agee called *Stage Door Canteen* "a preview of a period piece," adding that "any film is, but this one carries a saturation of the mannerisms of fourth-decade entertainment, patriotism, and sub-idealized lovemaking which could supply almost any twenty others." Stylization, however, was not alone at the heart of a "dream." In this review Agee added that "every piece of entertainment, like every political speech or swatch of advertising copy, has nightmarish accuracy as a triple-distilled image of a collective dream, habit, or desire" (*Reviews*, p. 41); and in part of the Selznick review he had more or less itemized the elements of this "triple-distilled image":

Somebody, some day, must do a Tobacco Road *about the Hiltons, their habits and their home; they need it perhaps more than any other Americans. But until that or a still better day comes, I shall have as much respect as disrespect for Mr. Selznick's conception of them. He is not what I would call perceptive, for he is obviously, and I think disarmingly, in love with his*

subject. Since his subject is also in love with itself, this creative
attitude has its points. So far as conscious intention and percep-
tion last, it means a fidelity to detail—of properties, costumes,
voices, gestures—which the most detached of artists could not
hope to improve on. When the consciousness blurs into love, it
means fidelity to dream, easy enough to scorn unless you realize
that the Hiltons and their kind live as much in a dream of them-
selves as in anything one would venture to call "reality." [Re-
views, p. 107]

In speaking of a "triple-distilled image" Agee is essentially describing the eyes which see and evaluate a subject. In the case of
Since You Went Away, the first image is the director's: "he
is . . . in love with his subject." The second image is the subject's:
"his subject is also in love with itself." And the third image,
logically enough, is the audience's, seven out of ten of which,
Agee writes, "would sell their souls" for the Hilton home (*Reviews,* p. 107).

"Dream," then, is the term Agee gives to the influence of
values on consciousness, the influence of memory or emotions on
the act of perception. A "collective dream" is an expressed ag-
gregation of influenced perceptions. In a detailed letter to Archibald MacLeish, responding to a query for films produced during
the war suitable for collection in the Library of Congress, Agee
elaborated on the term:

Along the lines which are not essentially esthetic I would like
highly to recommend the strengthening and clarifying of one
angle for selection and study. . . . Roughly—perhaps even figura-
tively—I might define and recommend this as the attitude: that
the films be watched and analyzed and examined and preserved as
if they were dreams. For they are naive like dreams and, like
dreams, meaningful in ways more complex than the sociologist,
the moralist or the esthetician alone (or the psychoanalyst for
that matter) alone can discern, though the attitudes and tech-
niques of all of them would prove invaluable in the study . . .
films are collective dreams.[8]

Furthermore, both "poor" films, or films whose biases Agee disrespected, and "good" films, such as *The Birth of a Nation,* were "collective dreams." Of *Birth of a Nation* Agee wrote: "It seems to me to be a perfect realization of a collective dream of what the Civil War was like, as veterans might remember it fifty years later, or as children, fifty years later might imagine it" (*Reviews,* p. 313). As a collective dream, the film clarified and corroborated the dreams of its audience, their memories, or their imaginative expectations. On the other hand, the collective dream also reflected a radically subjective way of seeing reality, divulging the moral bias of the perceiver. Agee concludes his analysis of *Since You Went Away* with this assessment:

> *It is thus too, in their [the characters'] wonderful blend of acute authenticity and authentic self-delusion, that I accept most of the things the Hiltons and their friends do, not to mention Mr. Selznick's masterpiece, the Hilton home—one of those pitiful suburban brick things which is indeed the American home if you agree with me that seven out of ten Americans would sell their souls for it.* [Reviews, p. 107]

In Selznick's authenticity, Agee believes, he is authentically self-deluded. In his concern to represent the detail of such characters and of such a home, he expresses his moral evaluation of them and of his audience. It is not only that he "dreams" that these people and this home are good. It is that he "dreams" that his audience "dreams" the same. There is in his perception no respect for "otherness," but only a tacit assumption of "sameness," an ideal world refracted from the image of ideals, self-sustaining "but aesthetically self-defeating" (*Reviews,* p. 107) because it had no basis in what Agee takes to be reality.

Although the original aesthetic of *Famous Men,* to the effect reality reveals its own truth to the perceiver, was altered through the war years by a new emphasis—that a perceiver's values shape the truth revealed by reality—there is a consistent undercurrent in Agee's film criticism which is, in effect, a reflection of the major concern of modern consciousness: the breakdown of values assumed central to the Western tradition. *Let Us Now Praise Famous Men* had anticipated the "failure-of-nerve controversy," following Sidney Hook's article in the January-February 1943 issue of *Partisan Review*. Agee had already rejected the broad, humanistic assumption, defended by Hook, that science and reason were the basis of Western culture. In *Famous Men* he had already assumed the stance taken by Philip Wheelwright, who claimed that science could not completely answer for the phenomena of intuition, imagination, love, morality, and religion.[9] Yet the most obvious fiasco of scientific humanism was, if not the war itself, its culmination in the explosion of the atomic bombs over the Japanese cities of Hiroshima and Nagasaki. More than any other event of the war, the bombs shook Agee's very soul. "In what they said and did," he wrote in a little-noticed article, "Victory, the Peace: The Bomb," in *Time's* August 20, 1945 (96:19), issue:

men were still in the aftershock of a great wound, bemused and only semi-articulate, whether they were soldiers or scientists, or great statesmen, or the simplest of men. But in the dark depths of their minds and hearts, huge forms moved and silently arrayed themselves: Titans, ranging out of the chaos an age in which victory was already only the shout of a child in the street.

Following his belief that the splitting of the atom brought humanity and civilization "into a new age in which all thoughts and things were split—and far from controlled," Agee declared a deeply personal and almost raging conviction of faith:

When the bomb split open the universe and revealed the prospect of the infinitely extraordinary, it also revealed the oldest, simplest, commonest, most neglected and most important of facts: that each man is responsible for his own soul, and, in the terrible words of the Psalmist, that no man may deliver his brother, nor make agreement unto God for him.

Nevertheless, Agee's alienated subjectivity—reflected in his poetry at the time—was very similar to most Americans' in their reaction to war, the bomb, and the peace. He was blessed only by a broader sensibility than David Selznick (or most returning veterans), whose ideas of redemption were a good job, a happy home, and a Negro maid. For this reason the term "dream" can be found as often in Agee's own postwar lyrics as it can in his journalistic analyses. For example, in a poor and unfinished poem, "Marx, I agree . . . ", Agee writes:

Rivers inscribe their trees: the listing earth
Retires, restores, its halves upon the sun:
Continually I hear the shouts of birth,
The sighs of death, and I wish that I were done.

. . . .

Here, where the heart inherits nobler themes
Than hope and kindness ever bred before,
Yet must I drown beneath a depth of dreams
And never hope for any breathing more.

. . . .

All I care to live for is to show
These as they seem. To see, and not to say;
I do; and can't; is more than I can go,
Then God, God, why, why, do I stay. [10]

"Dreams" here imply more than mere artistic aspiration. "The sighs of death" are the "depth of dreams" beneath which the poet drowns. Thus artistic acts which the poet values are not only unfruitful, but even confusing or stifling. In another poem, "November 1945" (actually two sonnets), the term "dream" implies both artistic aspirations and the way in which the poet values experience:

I.

Now on the world and on my life as well,
Ancient in beauty, infant in such fear
As no time else had dreamed, nor shall dispel,
Loosen the ashes of another year.

Whether by nature's will, man's or my own,
I who by chance walked softly past a war
Shall not by any chance the world has known
Be here, and breathing, many autumns more.
Only, with all who in past worlds have died,
I had, till lately, faced my death secure,
Knowing my hunger only was denied;
All I most loved and honored would endure.
But this year, dying struck wild as it fell,
Ending itself, me, and the world as well.

II.

This being so, and thirty and five years
So nearly vanished, and so little used;
All delights turned as trivial as all tears,
All meanings altered and all hopes refused;
By what means shall I, in what little while
Abides my being, on such narrowed span
As will and world allow, find out that trial
Of strength wherethrough, well fought, I die a man?
O long, long, idle in tribulation
Grown fat in all I did because I must,
I dreamed at least I knew my own salvation:
Now I begin to wake, and it is dust.
Where is the Angel in whose rage alone
Wrestling, I live? The night is nearly gone. [11]

The title purposely recalls Agee's November birthdate, which he explained to Father Flye as "a kind of melancholy about my life, a sort of personal Day of Atonement" (*Letters*, p. 185). The fatalism of the first sonnet is explained by the oblique reference to the Atomic Bomb in its last two lines: "But this year, dying, struck wild as it fell,/Ending itself, me, and the world as well." The Bomb puts an end not only to his "hunger," but also to "all I most loved and honored," his evaluation of experience. The second sonnet indicates Agee's response to "all meanings altered and all hopes refused" to be like that of a wakened dreamer, and the last six lines of the poem compile a number of personal implications: that the poet "knew [his] own salvation," but because of his presumption he has grown "fat," "idle in tribulation"; and that from this dream he has begun "to wake, [but] it is dust."

For within this dream there is yet another, that of Jacob, the son favored by his mother, the thief of the birthright, the father of the twelve tribes, the dreamer who saw his progeny blessed by God and who wrestled all night with Him to secure the blessing. Reviewing his life, then, it seems to the poet a succession of dreams, moral concessions, and moral victories: that he would be a writer; that he had found the way to be a writer; that in being a writer he would achieve happiness as well as the salvation of his soul; and that those nights in which he often could not find sleep nor dreams as well as those in which, finding sleep, he found dreams, were "nearly gone."

Like the thrust of his remarks on war films, Agee's war poetry reflects his new attitude that consciousness is a state of dream. The ambiance of unfulfilled ambitions and semisuicidal compromises, of madness rampant in a maddeningly sane world, affected the Joycean clarity of the aesthetics with which he had begun the decade. The Bomb, he wrote in the *Time* article cited above, "created a bottomless wound in the living conscience of the race." By emphasizing the "living" as compared to Joyce's "uncreated" conscience of the race, Agee's feelings were consistent with the disgust and horror of realism which he had confessed to Father Flye while he was still at Exeter. The Bomb, he was declaring, was an affront to perception. He therefore began to use his poetry to investigate other areas of consciousness. In two poems written in 1946 Agee speaks of the dream consciousness of an unborn or sleeping child and the collective dream consciousness of dead soldiers. The concluding three stanzas of the first poem, perhaps written before the November 1946 birth of his daughter, Teresa, expresses the poet's apology for the world to an unborn or sleeping child:

If in your dreams you hear, forgive:
For by our doing you must live.

Soon you must wake, and dreams be done
When you behold the heavy sun.

Once you undertake that weight
Apologies will come too late. [12]

The relation between a possible dream consciousness before birth
and the dream consciousness of existence after birth, the words
of the "creator," either poet or father or in a larger sense God,
explaining the creature's fated responsibility to live, all these are
preludes to themes found in Agee's later autobiographical fiction.
A similar relationship between the dream of a living consciousness
and that of a consciousness after death is suggested in a poem
Agee quotes to Father Flye in a letter dated March 29, 1945. It
concerns dead or sleeping soldiers:

Asleep, perfected, you would never believe
Harm of one of them. That stirring hand,
That leg, might clasp, endear, be brought across
An enemy, as gently as a wife.
How God must grieve,
Watching in all this shadow land
The flinching vigil candles of this countless loss
In night's nave each a life:
Who groans, smiles, murmurs, quiets; then on the horn
Transpierced, assembles upward, and reborn,
By all that skill and bravery crowns him with
Works, while he wakes, to put himself to death.

[Letters, pp. 140–41]

The ambivalent suggestion here of death or life as a dream results
in the double irony of a resurrection or the simple waking to fight
to the death. The "horn," then, is that of judgment or reveille.
The soldiers are either "reborn" in life after death or by waking
from their sleep. Though God grieves both for their deaths and
for their lives that do the work of death, ironically He rewards
their bravery only with "works . . . to put [themselves] to
death."

Following the war, then, even God's love for creation seemed duplicitous to Agee. Forced to analyze the events of each week in *Time*, Agee could do little more than arrange the elements of the news while he privately wallowed in a kind of blinded and aimless self-pity. The shock of certain events, however—specifically the Bomb, his birthday, and Christmas—seemed to provide him with a special energy for definition. While his essays on returning veterans and on the Bomb were accurate prefaces to what is called "the Atomic Age," Agee's Christmas essay for 1945 was in addition a preface to the direction he would personally take. Since March of that year he, like many others, had been experiencing something of a religious revival. In writing *Time*'s Christmas essay, he posed the question of the significance of the Christ child in a world devastated by war and clinging to the scant hope of a nuclear peace:

> *He is all that each man knows in the best conscience of his own soul, and all that has the humility and the courage to try to act accordingly, without compromise, against no matter what pressures or inducements.*
>
> *A non-religious word for this is individualism. It is a special kind of individualism. It is not the kind which insists on getting its own way at the expense of others; it is the kind whose rule is, "Thou shalt love thy neighbor as thyself." It is not the kind which insists, or assumes, that the world, or any part of same, owes it a living, or a happy life, or for that matter anything else whatever, except a battleground on which to fight out its small personal epic between good and evil.*
>
> *Such an individual is unable to believe that mankind, if only he becomes reasonable enough, can work out a comfortable life for himself. He knows too well the power of evil and of mere weakness in his own self to doubt its existence in others; and he knows that reason itself is capable of its own forms of self-deceit, and is defenseless against them.* [13]

In the birth of Christ, then, Agee sought to reaffirm the values of brotherly love and self-responsibility which he had assumed to be at the basis of Western civilization and which he profoundly believed to have been defiled by the horrors of the Second World War and the Atomic Bomb. Finding himself in conflict with the societal values of efficiency, mechanization, and materialism, his aesthetics, which proclaimed the "dignity of actuality," no longer seemed to him completely adequate. The poetry he wrote toward the end of the war expressed despair for his own "forms of self-deceit." But beyond that, the unpublished draft of this Christmas essay indicates his desire to probe the source of his own values and to recognize the significance of the Christ child's birth within himself. This impulse was to give birth to the second and last flowering of his creative power, the attempt to reclaim himself and restate his heritage through autobiographical fiction.

In the top righthand corner of a scrap of brown newsprint found among his papers Agee had written the word, "Bomb." Beneath it are three sentences in his crimped, miniscule hand:

> *This is the worst single event in history; and I should think also the greatest. We have it as immediately now as in our hands, to destroy ourselves, or to learn [how?] not to. There is no longer any possible alternative.*[1]

Father Flye recalls this as the gist of Agee's feelings when one evening in early August, 1945, he had stopped by Father Flye's summer apartment in Greenwich Village to ask him if he had been listening to the news. When his friend said he had not, Agee suggested he pour himself a good drink. "They've dropped an atomic bomb on the Japanese," he added grimly.[2] By the time Father Flye returned to St. Andrew's in the fall, Agee was writing him to say that he had begun a book as well as a "draft of a story . . . about the atomic bomb." Also he had started "a short novel about adolescence in the 1920's." Apparently Agee was trying to work out a schedule whereby he could do creative work three times a week, but he was having trouble adjusting to conflicts. "It seems possible to 'adjust' to anything short of atomic liquefaction," he noted sardonically, "and I'll probably keep right on adjusting" (*Letters*, p. 152).

In many ways this surprisingly cheerful letter is a scenario for the next five years of his life. The remaining paragraph centers around the questions implicit in his reaction to the bomb: "Supposing 2 to 25 years to go, what is worth doing and what is worth writing? . . . which is more important, survival or integrity?" (*Letters*, pp. 152–53). Another war, nuclear and final, is presumed. Coupled with this feeling is his sense of his approaching thirty-sixth birthday and his mistaken belief that his father died at that age. Under these and other pressures he was hearing "Time's winged chariot" and felt the urgency to finally make something of his life as an artist. Surviving would be simply avoiding nuclear holocaust. Integrity, on the other hand, would be to affirm the values of his forebears—"to touch with deathlessness their clay," as he had written in an early sonnet (*Poems*, p. 38, l. 13)—the artistic obligation under which he had labored for years, always in the face of an imagined death sentence. The book about the Bomb seems to have been lost. However, the story draft is most probably "Dedication Day. A Rough Sketch for a Moving Picture," which he finished before the end of the year and placed with Dwight Macdonald's new magazine, *Politics.*

Peter Ohlin seems entirely correct in saying there is nothing in "Dedication Day" to indicate that it is "a rough sketch for a moving picture" (Ohlin, p. 169). Nevertheless, several of Agee's story outlines, perhaps among them the "novel about adolescence in the 1920's," were initially projected for film treatment.[3] Although there are no notes for camera work, dialogue, or action, Agee might have wanted to give the narrator of "Dedication Day" a more subdued role as the commentator on a sound track. There is no discrepancy, however, in his posture as a sincere and all-too-innocent journalist. Indeed, the story's irony, like that of the later "A Mother's Tale," derives from the narrator. He reports, with affection only for the detail, a ceremony dedicating a monument to "the greatest of human achievements," the splitting of the atom. The finest, or what is considered the finest, talent has contributed to the event. The monument is in the form of an arch, designed by Frank Lloyd Wright. The ceremony—attended by no less than four Roman Catholic cardinals, "a group of eminent Protestant clergymen," and "the most prominent and progressive of American Reformist Rabbis"—is counterpointed by a televised performance of the choral movement from Beethoven's Ninth Symphony, conducted by Arturo Toscanini, "in a new translation by Louis Aragon and Harry Brown, done under the supervision of Robert E. Sherwood." The climax is reached when "the healthiest three-year-old in the United States," a girl named

Lidice (after the Czechoslovakian village razed by the Nazis in reprisal for Heydrich's assassination) lights the monument's "eternal fuse" (p. 121). Agee's reporter covers every detail of this ceremony in what J. Douglas Perry has called "a horribly apt kind of ingenuity." Perry relates it to such diverse works as Hawthorne's "The Celestial Railroad," Mark Twain's "Speech on Accident Insurance," and Nathaniel West's description of Wu Fong's international stable of prostitutes in *A Cool Million* (Perry, p. 167). Agee's approach is not unlike the "fidelity to detail" he had noted in the dream-conscious Selznick film, *Since You Went Away.*

There is only one "pathetic incident" to mar "the otherwise perfect day." An elderly scientist who had helped develop the Bomb seeks some way to atone for his "sin." At first he asks to share the fate of the maimed veterans and Japanese bomb victims who manufacture the fuse beneath the arch "in a small, air-conditioned ventilated workshop so ingeniously contrived by Norman Bel Geddes." Unfortunately his self-recriminations attract the attention of too many tourists who visit the workshop, impairing the "intended dignity, charm and decorum of the exhibit." As a final request before his release, he asks to throw the switch to fire the fuse on the day of dedication. The demand is granted, and the scientist commits suicide "as, indeed, a kind of religious or ethical 'sacrifice,' through which he hoped to endow the triumphal monument with a new and special significance." Like any sacrifice, the death provokes a reaction. Psychoanalysts probe his motivation. Philosophers conduct a symposium "to be entitled *The New New Failure of Nerve.*" And clergymen decide to preach on the text; "Render unto Caesar the things that are Caesar's, and unto God the things that are God's." Agee's reporter, while admitting that the scientist's last days were "misguided," suggests that

. . . . *he was nevertheless, perhaps, our last link with a not-too-distant past in which such conceptions as those of "atonement", and "guilt," and "individual responsibility," still had significance.*

And, in a sense, his gift to mankind was greater, perhaps, than that of his more stable colleagues. For, though "sacrifice" is a word to be used only with apologies, it would be hard to define what, if anything they "sacrificed" in the giving; but he gave up his sanity. [pp. 123-25]

Although "Dedication Day" lacks the finished development of either its narrator or his subject, it remains a sophisticated and complex satire in its treatment of collective as against individual responsibility. Part of the impetus for the story can be found in Agee's temperament: "there is little that I will render to Caesar beyond taking care at intersections," he had written Father Flye in 1940 (*Letters*, p. 125). However, a more immediate provocation can be found in an article he wrote for the "Religion" section of the October 15, 1945, issue of *Time*, (pp. 62-64). The news summary of religious reaction to the dropping of the Bomb was entitled "Godless Götterdämmerung." The key commentary in the article, however, was provided by Dwight Macdonald, who had written in *Politics* to the effect that the soldiers and scientists who had created and used the Bomb had done so with little knowledge of its effects. "They thought of themselves as specialists," Agee quotes Macdonald, "not as complete men." Perhaps Macdonald had raised this question in regards to Agee's scientist, for in writing Macdonald about "Dedication Day" Agee had commented; "I don't entirely like the scientist either." Although the "Dedication Day" reporter suggests an amoral atmosphere—"it was not clear either to the speakers or to the listeners precisely why or to what purpose or idea the Arch had been raised" ("DD," p. 121)—Agee's major moral statement concerns the scientist's suffering and courage rather than his lack of integrity or wholeness. What the story misses, perhaps, is the very quality for which Lionel Trilling had faulted *Famous Men*—a failure of moral realism, or Agee's inability to see the scientist "as anything but good." Here Trilling's criticism seems more appropriate, because Agee's reporter, unlike his persona in *Famous Men*, does not accept the moral burden of the drama. He is as unresponsive as the people about whom he is writing.

In reviewing American literature concerning the Bomb, Kingsley Widner has argued that it demonstrates a "failure of imagination," an inability to evaluate the event.[4] Agee's writing represents an exception to this rule. "Dedication Day," the only creative piece concerning the Bomb which saw print in Agee's lifetime, is a ruthlessly hyperbolic evaluation of the event as well as the culmination of a series of comments on society and the individual stemming out of Agee's Southern background. Although he was not old enough—nor did he have any such inclination—to join the Southern Agrarians, he shared some basic impulses with them. His early satires at Exeter were typically twentieth-century Southern in their bemused contempt for industrialization and commercialism. His play, "Catched," portrays the unique economic trap in which Tennessee mountaineers, especially women, are caught. All this work stresses human culpability, rather than environmental determinants—the evils of technology or capitalism. As he grew older, his viewpoint broadened. For one thing, in much of his Exeter work he, like many poets of that time throughout the country, was searching for a mythic or cultural synthesis. For another, he was trying to clarify to himself the quality of the life he had left in Tennessee in order that he might contrast it with and understand the quality of the life he was living in New England. By the time he revisited the South on assignment for *Fortune* in the summer of 1933, a conflux of causes and effects—the Depression, the New Deal's attempt at economic reform, and most importantly, his own latent memories of the South and his people—fused in his mind. *Fortune* readers may have thought that he was generalizing, but the mountaineers he is discussing in the following paragraph could have been, in fact, his grandparents:

He is the strong backbone of the Tennessee Valley. His forefathers settled this country in the 1700's when the effete civilization east of the Alleghenies stuck in their craws. They whipped the Britishers and Loyalists at Kings' Mountain. They kept much to themselves and their great-grandsons do likewise and live in much the same way, while slowly the sawmills and the mines and

the railways and the highways and now TVA burn seclusion from
about them. Many of them are illiterate; many are lawless in the
bad sense and the good of that word. They never heard of Mar-
garet Sanger and they have little interest in Mazda bulbs and little
respect for this century of progress. Homespun and feuds and
"mountain dew" are not so rife among them as some dreamy
souls would have you believe, but you would find them all if you
looked around a bit. Their language is pidgin-Elizabethan and
some of their sons are still of the sea and of England and strong in
blood in a species of individualism which makes the Gary brand
look more pallid than usual. In short, for all the cheap romancing
the fact has had, they are of that incomparably pure American
stock which produced such men as Lincoln and Chief Justice
Marshall, and, for that matter, Cordell Hull. TVA has a deep but
realistic respect for what it calls the native culture of the valley
and, far more directly than the citizens of Knoxville, the mount-
aineer is a part of TVA's plans. ["The Project is Important,"
Fortune *8 (October 1933):88]*

The overwhelming purport of this passage is its definition of the
dignity of Southern individualism and the quality of a certain
segment of Southern life, shortly to be affected by the far-reach-
ing hands of technology. None of this was lost—was, in fact,
reasserted and enhanced—in Agee's treatment of sharecroppers in
Let Us Now Praise Famous Men. But there he was still writing
about the mystery, and not the problem, of individuals. Ultimately he did not believe that simplistic efforts at economic or social
reform would significantly affect the values of the mountaineers'
or the tenants' lives. He was much more concerned with the
mysterious design of chance which made a tenant a tenant and a
journalist a journalist. By 1945, however, his viewpoint had altered. The Second World War had demonstrated to him the hide-
ous as well as the anesthetic effects of mechanization, and what
he was to detail in notes for another film satire about the Bomb,
written shortly after "Dedication Day," was to be remarkably
similar to the Agrarian tenets which had been reiterated in 1939
by Donald Davidson.

Writing an explication of the second collection of Agrarian essays, *Who Owns America?*, Davidson restated the thesis operative in that book and in the earlier *I'll Take My Stand*. "Under industrialism," he wrote, "no man sees the end of his deed, no man faces the consequences of his act. And not knowing the end of his deed, he is precluded from becoming a moral agent."[5] Some similar sensibility is clear behind Agee's reaction to war documentaries. In a fragment of an article essentially containing his 1945 reaction to the documentary, Agee had written that the process of watching films of actual and horrifying events places the viewer "in a strange, sterile, helpless relation to overwhelming images of a certain kind of truth."[6] In this instance he views the machine not as a medium of, but a hindrance to, truth, which suggests that his commitment to minimal transformational art during and following the publication of *Famous Men* was in response to similar feelings. However, closer parallels to Davidson's "law of distant consequences," as well as to Agrarian individualism, can be found in the notes and rough drafts of a film satire Agee wrote, probably in 1947, with Charlie Chaplin in mind for the hero. The story concerns the survivors of a nuclear attack, one group of which is technologically and scientifically minded while another—inspired by Chaplin's tramp figure—is humanitarian. For this latter segment Agee devises a quasiutopian society, based on barter, where "necessities are taken care of with considerable seriousness."[7] In fact, the close relationship between a man and his work in this community is an accurate reflection of Davidson's law:

No mechanical principle is used that does not finally depend on the strength of the body or the skill of the hand; there are for instance, no engines; nothing is power-driven. It is explained that there is nothing intrinisically evil about machinery . . . but that once they are admitted, chain-reactions seem inevitably to set in which get far beyond human control. Plenty of people remember, wistfully, the pleasures of auto-driving, for instance. But the machine of even one auto, and the use of power, involves too many people to be good in the long run, for each individual involved.

And *though machines are neither good nor evil, much is lost when personal skill and strength are* lost. People *begin to group too largely, and to depend on groups, rather than on themselves and on each other* as *individuals. And that is always bad.*

Essentially the themes of this brilliant but unfinished satire of cold war America, given the title "Scientists and Tramps" by Victor Kramer when he published a synopsis in 1968, can be found in the articles Agee wrote for *Time* in the latter half of 1945. His major concern in the film, stated above in conclusion to the news article "Godless Götterdämmerung," is that people no longer act responsibly because they see themselves, not as individuals, but as members of a group, where responsibility is either shared or avoided.

Agee's method, however, is almost identical to the pattern he had established in "The House." He begins by satirizing contemporary persons and institutions, editing in film clippings which juxtapose the Japanese surrender aboard the *Missouri* with shots of bomb survivors and "a staggering Baker Day goat." Then there is a cataclysm which destroys everything, leaving Agee free to create a new society literally in the ashes of the old. Although the treatment of "Scientists and Tramps" is more controlled than was the earlier script, Agee's utopian solution remains the same: society is left in the hands of its children or of childlike individuals. The impulse, of course, is romantic, but in Agee's case it has a historical significance. It is more than the nostalgia Wright Morris finds common to American writers, more than the loss of Eden which is the subject of R. W. B. Lewis's *The American Adam.*[8] For in 1945 there was not merely a sense of evil in the world—a feeling that loved ones died, that justice was ill-served, that mankind was ubiquitously vicious; there was also a very palpable sense of despair, the conviction that there was no "territory ahead" and that no matter what good course could be advised, it no longer mattered because the world would shortly be obliterated. Only within this historical context can Agee's 1945 Christmas essay be properly understood to carry the message that everyone must recognize the child within himself. Only within this context can we finally appreciate Agee's note concerning the Chaplin figure in "Scientists and Tramps"; "I am sure of it, that people coming slowly together out of shock and horror and finding this childlike man, surviving bravely and well, could rediscover the childishness in themselves, and live accordingly." For Agee is not endorsing a return to an Edenic innocence; it must be remembered that he believed too strongly in the doctrine of Original Sin. In the draft of his Christmas essay he had written that the individualism signified by the Christ child "is unable to believe that mankind, if only he becomes reasonable enough, can work out a comfortable life for [itself]." Life was nothing more than a battleground upon which an individual can "fight out its small personal epic between good and evil." Essentially Agee's Tramp Community is devised in order to allow for life after the Fall. It emphasizes personal enjoyment or fulfillment, but there is also evil—that is, physical corruption and human limitation. Every effort is made, simply, "to prevent its getting leverages of great power." In fact, it is on behalf of this effort that the Tramp is finally ostracized, for even the power of his goodness can take advantage of people. Agee's rediscovery of the child, then, is a recollection of an almost specific place and point in time—"Knoxville: Summer of 1915." It is not because life was any simpler then, though in his memory it might have been, but because people seemed to Agee to have lived then according to values which gave significance to their being alive. Agee sensed that the Bomb and the implications of the ensuing cold war had robbed him of his significance. In sum, the trend of his writing during this most creative period of his life was an attempt to find his worth. He never expressed the pertinence of the child in this respect better than in the rough drafts of his review of Chaplin's *Monsieur Verdoux*:

There is a devil in each of us, and a more or less crippled angel as well, and of the marriage of the two, a child more wonderful than either; and a home, a small and lovely nation at war; and more grimly perhaps than ever before, the need to defend it, the need of an expeditionary force. No one can avoid acting as an

expeditionary force, and no one can avoid the temptations, and
the possibilities of self-deceit, to which Verdoux succumbs.[9]

ii

One of Agee's few surviving attempts at fiction after college is "1928 Story," an unfinished manuscript resembling in some respects an outline for three related plots projected for film. Each of these stories as well as "1928 Story" concerns "adolescence in the 1920's." Hence it is reasonable to suppose, that "1928 Story" is the beginning of the novel he had mentioned to Father Flye in his letter of November 1945. The story concerns Irvine, a writer just returned from the war, and his attempts to recover moments of his past life which seem to him genuine and alive. He finds himself playing old phonograph records. But he is confused as to what he is doing or why. His wife's reaction to the records is very different from his, and

it seemed quite possible, for that matter, that he was using them
as a way of retreating from her, and from everything else. He felt
that he had no business doing it, to her, or for that matter to
himself. He had to get used to living in the world again, after all.
And when he thought of it all he realized that the world he had
once lived in, and could never live in again, and that could never
again exist, was no great loss, to him or anyone else. [Texas
Quarterly, *p. 23]*

Irvine believes that he might be able to penetrate the anesthesia of his times if he were to write about it, but he does not have the heart to even try. A poem of his which his wife had submitted during the war to *Partisan Review* had been accepted and published. But a letter he had received from a "good poet" and editor, though complimentary, had reflected a disheartening sophistication in its reaction "to the disturbing hint in lines 4–7 that Irvine was beginning perhaps to take a polite interest in God" (p. 25). Thus the chief reason Irvine distrusts the work of his contemporaries is that, despite their surface adroitness, they are not filled with any deep convictions. They seem like so many "overliterate 'sensitive' middle-class boys with a great deal of adolescent excitement and a certain facility of the senses and with words and forms" (p. 25). Although Irvine admits that the difference between him and them is, simply, "that they had kept on producing" or that they had remained "adolescent" while he had "grown up" (p. 25), even those artists he held in contempt, Melville and Coleridge, had "in themselves that confidence that they at least, no matter about the others, were true artists, which for all his own years-long stultification, he could not get rid of" (p. 26).

Throughout this introspection Irvine is making an equation between adolescence and confidence, implying another equation between confidence and production. Obviously, then, "1928 Story" relates importantly to Agee's despair in 1932, when he could not write poetry and told Father Flye of his feeling that poetry was the "product of adolescence—or of an emotionally adolescent frame of mind." To reinforce his feelings, Irvine remembers an incident in his own adolescence, a morning during a summer vacation in Maine when he had a story that he could truthfully call "carefully written" (p. 26). As he had finished it, he poured himself a drink and placed "West Side Blues" on the record player. His memory of the music brings him back to the present, but listening to the

delicate, passionate music through, now, in a strange state of mind: perfectly, fiber by fiber, in cold and helpless regret; perfectly, at the same time, recalling, re-experiencing, the best that he had ever heard in it. [p. 27]

The music now recalls associations of confidence which fill Irvine with regret. His regret works against his ability to recall "the best that he had ever heard in it." And his ability to recall the excellence of the music is analogous to his ability to recall or reexperience or, finally, to represent the actual intensity of any emotion. Further, when Irvine had first heard the music, he had compared its lyrical qualities to Mozart's. But his mother and father's patronizing bemusement had led him to self-recriminations for ever having tried to share his feelings with them, and at length he defends his sensitivity by remembering his "new motto . . . 'silence, exile and cunning' " (p. 28).

Irvine's reflections here are somewhat similar to those of the narrator of Agee's college story, "They That Sow." He believes in the integrity of his emotional responses but finds himself at a loss to represent them. However, Irvine's withdrawal into Dedalus's artistic pose implies a different turn for Agee's art in 1945 than it would have in 1931. The music of *West Side Blues* leads Irvine to imagine "a place he had never known," an all-night café where Negro musicians jam throughout the night; and the details of this scene, which accumulate with each review, are less important to him than is his ability to conjure them. This process describes Agee's sure inclination toward the creation of fiction and suggests an answer to J. Douglas Perry's question of why, after affirming in his work that the camera was "the central instrument of our time," Agee turned to writing fiction instead of making films in the late 1940s (Perry, p. 139). Victor Kramer has also noted in reading Agee's story outlines concerning "adolescence in the 1920's" that they state explicitly that some aspects of reality are "less clearly shaped and more psychologically entangled," and thus the printed word can sometimes suggest a complexity of emotion and situation "not ammenable to movie treatment." ["Agee in the Forties," pp. 14–15] The possibility of treating psychological complexities, as well as his own need to affirm the imaginative process, seem to be the predominant aesthetic reasons Agee remained a writer. It might be suspected that in his characterization of Irvine, he was wrestling with one aspect of the question—the validity of the imaginative process—for the story seems to give him a tentative answer. As Irvine begins to doubt the existence of the café, its authenticity, his ability to describe it—all the doubts which had plagued Agee in writing *Let Us Now Praise Famous Men*—he only becomes convinced that if the café "didn't exist, it ought to, and that suited him" (p. 30).

The remainder of "1928 Story" is intended as an ironic rejoinder to this definition of imagination. In a Joycean episode Irvine goes swimming, sees a girl at a beach, and cannot get her out of his mind. He spies on her at night, smells her wet bathing suit on the clothes line, then catches a glimpse of her picking her nose. "God, Irvine thought: she's wonderful!" (p. 36). This scene provokes him to write a poem about the girl who emerges from the sea. "He had seldom written a worse poem," Agee writes. "But he did not destroy it" (p. 37). Thus despite the irony with which Agee comments on the poor quality of work resulting from Irvine's new-found belief in his imagination, he has actually and tacitly admitted that a conviction about the integrity of an emotion as well as its imaginative projection resides at the heart of any good writing. Certainly the concern of "1928 Story," the loss of a reality through the dying of sensations, is one of Agee's major artistic statements. It was always paramount for him to record his response to reality exactly, for it was the only way he had of capturing, of freezing the object of perception in memory. During the 1930s he was wary of letting this response assume an imagined shape, as he had, for instance, in "The House." Yet in writing "1928 Story," it seems that he found, or at least finally admitted, that as an emotion takes an imagined shape, a writer can be filled with a newer and fresher emotional response, which does not necessarily distort but can contribute to the integrity of the object. This process, as Victor Kramer has observed in studying the rough drafts and notes to *A Death in the Family* and *The Morning Watch,* is central to the composition of both novels. "In notes for each of these books," Kramer writes, "Agee himself raised questions of how he might catch the immediacy of a felt emotion with the phrase, 'a form of quasi poetry?' " (Kramer, p. 93). He had suggested years earlier, in regard to his narrative poetry, that it was a "clothesline on which to string my lyrics"; the process by which he later wrote his major fiction was to create a verbal situation to which he could respond integrally. And because the subject of these books is his own past, his response is tantamount to his survival as an individual.

Agee expressed the impulses which led to his autobiographical fiction in a section of the composite manuscript for *A Death in the Family* not included in the posthumously published version. Later published under the title "Dream Sequence," the manuscript strongly suggests the same postwar era Irvine is recalling in "1928 Story." It also bears thematic resemblances to two sonnets Agee published in 1950 in *Botteghe Oscure* and two fragments later published by Robert Fitzgerald.[10] Most of these manuscripts corroborate the allusions in Agee's letters to Father Flye, indicating that *A Death in the Family* was written between the autumns of 1947 and 1949.[11] Dwight Macdonald states that Agee left his jobs as film critic for *Time* and *The Nation* in the late summer of 1948 specifically to finish the novel.[12] The date is important, because most critics have assigned the composition to a time closer to Agee's death in 1955 and to the eventual publication in 1957. However, this placement distorts an accurate picture of Agee's development as an artist, for it does not take into account the important fact that his novel grew out of his reaction to the Bomb and the latent despair of the cold-war era. Furthermore, it gives the false impression that Agee's talent was improving at the end of his life, when in fact it was in decline.

Nothing reveals this relationship more clearly than a reading of "Dream Sequence," which Kramer suspects to have been intended as Agee's introduction to *A Death in the Family*. The manuscript, very possibly a recollection of one of Agee's own dreams, opens in the lunch hour in what the dreamer-narrator takes to be Chattanooga before he realizes "he was back home, in Knoxville" (*Texas Quarterly;* p. 38). A short walk from the station he can see a crowd which has killed a man. Despite his fear that the people might turn on him, he walks toward them. Almost instinctively he knows that the victim is John the Baptist and that he is obliged to bury him. He is also aware, however, that John was a partisan killed by partisans and that he himself is neutral. "Neverthelsss," he reasons, "he could only think ill of himself for his inevitable but convenient lack of convictions, as he looked down at the dead man; and this perhaps gave him more courage than he might otherwise have had" (p. 39). The narrator, then, carries the body through the hostility of downtown Knoxville, past the church in which he had been confirmed, to a vacant lot he remembers. But he miscalculates the streets and arrives at the wrong place. He puts the body down to rest, and when he returns to carry it to the correct piece of ground, the smell overwhelms him. Overcoming his nausea, he drags the body by its heels. Throughout his walk he notices that people watch him with an "interest . . . so strangely out of ratio to the thing they were looking at" that it seems "a measure of the commonness, by now of just such things, mob murders, corpses of heroes dragged through the streets" (p. 43). When they reach the resting ground, John's head becomes detached from his body. The narrator squats to pick it up and watches it curl "swiftly upon itself like a jellyfish, an armadillo, with a shape roughly like a catcher's mitt. . . . Sharing its escape with both hands," the dreamer lifts "the cold and gritty weight as if it were a Grail" (p. 44) just before he wakes.

He immediately tries to interpret the dream: the church in which he had been confirmed was St. John the Baptist; the corner to which he had brought the body was where he and his father had sat together in the evenings; "and his father had come out of the wilderness, and it was there that the Son had best known his homesickness for the wilderness" (p. 45). When he attempts to make the parallels between his father and John the Baptist and himself and Christ, however, he doubts "so thoroughly that the true meaning of any dream could ever be known" (p. 45). At the heart of his experience, he feels guilt, his responsibility for the head detaching from the dragged body:

I've betrayed my father, he realized. Or myself. Or both of us. How?

He thought of his father in his grave, over seven hundred miles away, and how many years. If he could only talk with him. But he knew that even if they could talk, they could never come at it between them, what the betrayal was. . . .

He thought of all he could remember about his father and about his own direct relations with him. He could see nothing which even faintly illuminated his darkness, nor did he expect ever to see anything, yet if he could be sure of anything except betrayal and horror, he could be sure that that was where the dream indicated that he should go. He should go back into those years. As far as he could remember; and everything he could remember; nothing he had learned or done since; nothing except (so well as he could remember) what his father had been as he had known him, and what he had been as he had known himself, and what he had seen with his own eyes, and supposed with his own mind.

The more he thought of it the surer he became that there was nothing he could hope to understand out of it which was not already obvious to him. All the same, he could make the journey, as he had dreamed the dream, for its own sake, without trying to interpret; and if the journey was made with sufficient courage and care, very likely that of itself would be as near the answer as he would ever hope to get. [p. 45]

This passage is clearly central to an understanding of Agee's reaction to the mood of the late 1940s. Like Irvine, the dreamer lacks conviction and seeks to find it in his past. Yet unlike much of the fiction of the 1940s which shared the same impulse, Agee's dreamer does not fault the society so much as he does himself. Victor Kramer is certainly correct in stating that "the death, the absence, and the 'betrayal' of the father all seem to be related to the disappointments of the dreamer with his contemporary world" (Kramer, pp. 103–04). However, the betrayal of the father is only a specific instance of the dreamer's feeling that he has betrayed his native culture. At the beginning of "Dream Sequence" the dreamer is glad to be home even while he is aware that Southerners would hate him "if they knew his mind." He further knows that he has inherited his loose stride "from the mountains," but that he is walking a little too quickly for Knoxville. In fact, his "lack of conviction"—or the other side of the same coin, his ability to see every aspect of a subject and commit

himself to none, his intellectual sophistication—was the penalty
he had paid for leaving home. Of course the dreamer realizes that
nothing can be changed. Yet the testimony of the past can be
given, "for its own sake, without trying to interpret"; and if it is
done well enough, so that once more the dreamer can catch a
glimpse of the dream, then "very likely that of itself would be as
near the answer as he would ever hope to get."

In many respects these are Agee's own reasons for writing *A
Death in the Family*. The characters of the hand-written draft are
given the names of Agee's family; and in accompanying notes
Agee writes that his intention is to tell of "my relation with my
father and, through that, as thorough as possible an image of him:
winding into other things on the way but never dwelling on
them." Further down on this page he expanded the entry in what
Victor Kramer thinks might have been Agee's outline for the
book:

Detachedly:

*A soft and somewhat precocious child. A middle-class religious
mother. A father of country background. Two sets of relatives:
hers middle class, northern born, more or less cultivated; his, of
the deep mountain country.*

*Begin with the complete security and the simple pleasures and
sensations.*

*Develop: the deficiency in the child which puts them at odds:
the increasing need of the child for the father's approval.*

*Interrupt with the father's sudden death. Here either the whole
family is involved, or it is told in terms of the child.*

*At end: the child is in a sense & degree doomed, to religion &
to the middle class. The mother: to religiosity. New strains develop, or are hinted between her & her family.* [13]

More must be understood, however, in order to take Kramer's
suggestion seriously. Foremost is the inescapable fact that the
manuscript is far from finished. In May 1950 Agee wrote to
Father Flye that he thought he could finish the book that summer (*Letters*, p. 181). That he repeated the same estimate five

years later in his last letter to Father Flye and also nights before his death to his friend and publisher David McDowell, suggests that he got little further in the writing. Kramer and others have pointed out that, in addition to the incomplete state of the manuscript, the published version is in need of reediting. [14] It is obvious that if the above note is taken as a possible outline for the novel, Agee had in mind much more than his relationship with his father. Indeed, he intended a history of the most formative years of his life, which would possibly explicate his "deficiency" or the manner in which he had "betrayed" his father. Other notes for the novel indicate that Agee was toying with a very complex plot, involving a network of misunderstandings involving every member of the family. Essentially the father, "at an uneasy time of his life," was trying to get ahead in his job. His purchase of an automobile—a chapter which Agee wrote but which was excluded from the published version—was symptomatic of his ambition. "He is progressive," Agee had noted. "In a sense it is this which kills him." [15] Unfortunately, though, these notes can only suggest the broad outlines of Agee's ideas. Although they indicate the direction of his reaction to the contemporary world, as well as implying the values he sought to restore to consciousness through his art, they can inevitably be supported only by reference to unfinished or unpublished manuscripts or to his more explicit statements in forgotten issues of *Time*.

What remains and has been published is perhaps little more than half the novel Agee intended to write. The twenty chapters and six italicized interchapters ("several scenes outside the time span of the basic story," editor McDowell explains in his headnote) tell the story of Jay Follet's death. Much of the action is seen from the point of view of his six-year-old son, Rufus. But a great deal goes on outside the boy's perception or experience. The novel begins when he and his father spend an evening watching a double feature of Chaplin and William S. Hart movies. But after Rufus is put to bed, Jay is called home to his own father, who is thought to be dying. On the way back a cotter pin comes loose from the steering column of his car, and he is killed instantly. The remaining two parts of the novel concern the grief of Mary, his widow, and the funeral and burial—actions which swirl largely above Rufus' head.

As Agee saw it, his main problem in writing the story was to

decide between a completely detached and deeply subjective treatment.

I doubt if in complete detachment there is a story there. Rather, do the subjective, as detachedly as possible. [16]

The outcome of these difficult instructions is remarkably similar to Agee's youthful ideal of abnormal sympathy and perfect balance. A good example of the result can be found in the shifting viewpoint Agee utilized in one of the best-known scenes of the novel, the seeming apparition of Jay's ghost to the family assembled in the Follet parlor:

Can't eat your cake and have it, his father thought.

Like slapping a child in the face, Andrew thought; he had been rougher than he had intended.

"But Andrew dear," Mary was about to say, but she caught herself. What a thing to argue about, she thought; and what a time to be wrangling about it!

Each of them realized that the others felt something of this; for a little while none of them had anything to say. Finally Andrew said, "I'm sorry." [Death, p. 148]

The subject of the passage is a remark about belief by Andrew, Mary's brother. There follows each character's reaction to the remark. This is a montage, a juxtaposition of viewpoints managed similarly to Joyce's technique in *Ulysses.* But Agee's style, unlike Joyce's, merges more than one subjective point of view and does not simply borrow from the film. Cinematic montage depends on the spatial relationship of visual details. Agee's shifting viewpoint can refer to visual details, but in this passage each element of response is a thoroughly subjective use of verbal expression: Mary's father, Joel, is given to cliché ("Can't eat your cake and have it"), Andrew to metaphor ("Like slapping a child"), Mary to half-thought ("But Andrew dear"), all followed by interior monologue ("What a thing to argue about"), and finally the authorial voice ("Each of them realized that the others felt something of this"). By detaching authorial control from the subjectivity of his characters, Agee has created a sense of presence rather than engaging in presentation.

This scene in which the family members grope to comfort one another also presents the essential drama of the novel, the interaction between loneliness and contentment. Agee introduces the theme in the first chapter, when Jay and Rufus pause for a moment on their way home from the movies. As they rest, Rufus begins to feel a kind of contentment because he senses no difference or estrangement between himself and his father:

> He felt also that although his father loved home and loved all of them, he was more lonely than the contentment of this family love could help; that it even increased his loneliness, or made it hard for him not to be lonely. He felt that sitting out here, he was not lonely; or if he was, that he felt on good terms with the loneliness; that he was a homesick man, and that here on the rock, though he might be more homesick than ever, he was well. He knew that a very important part of his well-being came of staying a few minutes away from home, very quietly, in the dark, listening to the leaves if they moved, and looking at the stars; and that his own, Rufus' own presence, was fully as indispensable to this well-being, and of the reasons for it, and knew how each depended on the other, how each meant more to the other, in this most important of all ways, than anyone or anything else in the world; and that the best of this well-being lay in this mutual knowledge, which was neither concealed nor revealed. [Death, pp. 22–23]

Essentially loneliness is estrangement, and in *A Death in the Family* it is often treated as a state of moral susceptibility. Contentment, on the other hand, is the tacit assumption and sharing of certain values and is seen most often as a state of moral redemption. Andrew apologizes for his remark about belief because he has upset Mary. But he has also estranged himself from the group, and his apology brings him back into their common concern for Mary. Another example can be found in the scene where Joel and Catherine Lynch, Mary's parents, are waiting for news of Jay. Catherine announces that despite their prior feelings about Jay, they must now care for him and Mary in their trouble. "Certainly," Joel replies. Then he

began to realize the emotion, and the loneliness behind the banality of what she had said; he was ashamed of himself to have answered as if it were merely banal. He wished he could think what to say that would make up for it. [Death, p. 111]

As Joel and Catherine act alone, the personal significance they attach to their words is not communicated, and the failure is apparent to each. But as they make a gesture toward one another, they restore the moral harmony.

She felt his hand on her wrist and his head close to hers. She leaned towards him.

"I understand, Catherine," he said.

What *does he mean that he understands, Catherine wondered. Something I failed to hear, no doubt, she thought, though their words had been so few that she could not imagine what. But she quickly decided not to exasperate him by a question; she was sure of his kind intention, and deeply touched by it. [Death, p. 111]*

When Mary's aunt Hannah is desperately trying to protect her niece from the ravages of her grief, she silently recoils from a suggestion to pray together: "Not yet, she wanted to say. For the first time in her life, she suspected how mistakenly prayer can be used" (*Death*, p. 104). And for the moment, Hannah is troubled by unbelief.

"Our Father," she heard herself say, in a strange voice; and Mary, innocent of her terror, joined in the prayer. And as they continued, and Hannah heard more and more clearly than her own the young, warm, earnest, faithful, heart-sick voice, her mo-

*ment of terrifying unbelief became a remembrance, a temptation
successfully resisted through God's grace. [Death, p. 105]*

Such individual instances of loneliness and contentment create
a general pattern, the random acts of individuals brought together
by human need. This pattern composes what Gerald Weales has
called the power of the novel: "Agee's unwavering knowledge
that each human being lives and moves in the loneliness of self,
but that the family, when infused with love, can occasionally,
almost accidentally, shore up that lonely self." [17] Weales' criticism is valuable especially for the concept of "accidental compassion." For it is as if by accident that Joel places his hand upon
Catherine's arm or that Hannah finds herself praying with Mary.
Accidental compassion, furthermore, is part of Mary's religious
faith. Religion is to her more than a ritual of comfort; it is the
experience by which she endures her husband's death. Her prayer
before sleep the night of Jay's death is, "If Thou, Lord, wilt be
extreme to mark what is done amiss O Lord, who may abide it?"
(*Death,* p. 160). Not only do the words bring the relief of tears in
the realization of the emptiness of her life without Jay, but the
accidental freedom with which she whispers them is dependent
upon her belief that the trials of human life are insuperable and
that God is therefore ultimately necessary. Similarly, it is an accident of compassion which is at the heart of Andrew's "conver-
sion" in the closing pages of the novel. Agee's notes indicate his
attempt to recall each detail of his father's funeral, "but mainly,"
he wrote, "I remember [my uncle's] needing to tell me about the
butterfly." [18] Not only is Andrew restored or "contented" by
asking Rufus to share his thoughts, but the cause of his contentment is the accidental flight of a butterfly off Jay's coffin as it is
lowered into the ground. The implication Andrew derives from
the butterfly is that God has made a gesture concerning Jay to
which he responds: " 'If there are any such things as miracles,' his
uncle said, as if someone were arguing with him, 'then that's
surely miraculous' " (*Death,* p. 252).

Significantly, Jay is seldom susceptible to loneliness. For him,
loneliness and contentment are one. Although Agee tells of the

difficulties of Jay and Mary's marriage—his drinking, their religious differences, the history of their separate values—Jay is both a part of and apart from the world of the other characters. As Rufus perceives in the novel's first chapter, Jay "was more lonely than the contentment of this family love could help." However, in nature—the empty lot, the journey to his father's home, the visit to his great-grandmother's homestead—Jay is "on good terms with the loneliness . . . though he might be more homesick than ever, he was well." The two instances in which loneliness threaten Jay support this reading. While deciding whether to drive to his father's house immediately after talking to his brother, Ralph, or to wait, as Mary wishes, until the morning, Jay thinks:

That's easy for you to say. He's not your father, and besides you've always looked down on him. But he drove this thought so well away that he thought ill of himself for having believed it, and said, "Sweetheart, I'd rather wait and see what we hear in the morning, just as much as you would. It may all be a false alarm. I know Ralph goes off his trolley easy. But we just can't afford to take that chance." [Death, pp. 28–29]

Similarly, though with a significant difference, Jay overcomes loneliness a second time while rocking Rufus to sleep.

Just one way, you do get back home. You have a boy or a girl of your own and now and then you remember, and you know how they feel, and it's almost the same as if you were your own self again, as young as you could remember.

And God knows he was lucky, so many ways, and God knows he was thankful. Everything was good and better than he could have hoped for, better than he ever deserved; only, whatever it was and however good it was, it wasn't what you once had been, and had lost, and could never have again, and once in a while, once in a long time, you remembered, and knew how far you were away, and it hit you hard enough, that little while it lasted, to break your heart.

He felt thirsty, and images of stealthiness and deceit, of open-

ness, anger and pride, immediately possessed him, and immediate-
ly he fought them off. If ever I get drunk again, he told himself
proudly, I'll kill myself. And there are plenty good reasons why I
won't kill myself. So I won't even get drunk again.

He felt consciously strong, competent both for himself and

against himself, and this pleasurable sense of firmness contended
against the perfect and limpid remembrance he had for a moment
experienced, and he tried sadly, vainly, to recapture it. But now
all that he remembered, clear as it was to him, and dear to him,
no longer moved his heart, and he was in this sadness, almost
without thought, staring at the wall, when the door opened softly
behind him and he was caught by a spasm of rage and alarm, then
of shame for these emotions. [Death, *pp. 76–77]*

The unresolved ironies of this monologue reveal the critical
·ore of the novel. Jay's plenty good reasons" rescue him from
the temptations of the loneliness he feels because of the loss of
his past, "what [he] once had been." Similarly, in "1928 Story"
Irvine's "maturity" allows him to realize the inadequacy of his
past adolescent confidence. Nevertheless, the search for the
"what you once had been" is the object of many of Agee's fictional characters. Perhaps the question of exactly what Jay feels
he has lost can never be answered. But remembering the significance of the Chaplin figure in "Scientists and Tramps," we may
suspect that the loss is nothing so simple as the disappearing
pristine innocence of an American Adam. Rather, the loss the
characters feel seems part of a strategy to reveal what Agee considers the fundamental paradox of the human condition. Such
was, for instance, the function of Irvine's loss in "1928 Story":
he believed in his adolescent confidence only insofar as Agee
could exploit it as an illusion.

Agee's characterization of Rufus serves the same end. Though
drawn along general lines, Rufus' delineation is specific enough to
render a credible character. He is imitative of his parent's and
elder's values. When he meets his Aunt Hannah to go shopping, he
repeats the formula his mother had given him: "I'm *very glad* to
come, Aunt Hannah, and thank you very much for thinking of

me" (*Death*, p. 61). When choosing a hat, he picks the one he is sure will be approved (*Death*, p. 65). But he can also be very discriminating. He knows why he appreciates his aunt: "of all grown people she was the most considerate" (*Death*, p. 63), and he knows that he dislikes Father Jackson, the priest who comes to pray at his father's funeral, for exactly the opposite reason. Rufus is likely to exhibit a very good mind discussing God with his mother (*Death*, p. 49), or cunningly tormenting his baby sister (*Death*, p. 51), or breaking his mother's rule in order to satisfy his curiosity about Negroes (*Death*, pp. 86–88). But his role in the novel seems greater than the portrayal of the young, sensitive son. In fact, Rufus' character is the clearest embodiment of the novel's theme of loneliness and contentment.

The interchapter which ends with Jay's monologue begins with Rufus' dream that turns into a nightmare. In the dream Rufus converses with darkness, which tells him it is a sheltering force; but soon darkness turns into a malevolent force:

Darkness indeed came near. It buried its eye against the eye of the child's own soul, saying:

Had ever breathed, had ever dreamed, had ever been.

And somewhat as in blind night, on a mild sea, a sailor may be made aware of an iceberg, fanged and mortal, bearing invisibly near, by the unwarned charm of its breath, nothingness now revealed itself: that permanent night upon which the stars in their expiring generations are less than the glinting of gnats, and nebulae, more trivial than winter breath; that darkness in which eternity lies bent and pale, a dead snake in a jar, and infinity is the sparkling of a wren blown out to sea; that inconceivable chasm of invulnerable silence in which cataclysms of galaxies rave mute as amber.

Darkness said:

When is this meeting, child, where are we, who are you, child, who are you, do you know who you are, do you know who you are, child; are you?

He knew that he would never know, though memory, almost captured, unrecapturable, unbearably tormented him. That this little boy whom he inhabited was only the cruelest of deceits. That he was but the nothingness of nothingness, condemned by some betrayal, condemned to be aware of nothingness. That yet in that desolation, he was not without companions. For featureless on the abyss, invincible, moved monstrous intuitions. And from the depth and wide throat of eternity burned the cold, delirious chuckle of rare monsters beyond rare monsters, cruelty beyond cruelty. [Death, pp. 68–69]

The darkness is all that is unknown. The dream is of security and shelter, which brings with it a sense of personal identity. The nightmare, however, is that the dream is false—further, that the identity which security and shelter provide is an illusion. What Jay is yearning for is actually the identity of Rufus' dream. Yet the paradox is that while Rufus' dream compels belief, it is an unmistakable deceit.

The paradox of dream and nightmare, of desire and illusion, finally culminates in Rufus' feelings during his walk with his Uncle Andrew, following his father's burial. Rufus' initial reaction to Andrew's story about the butterfly is one of pride in sharing the confidence of his uncle, a source of contentment and security.

He could see it very clearly, because his uncle saw it so clearly when he told about it, and what he saw made him feel that a special and good thing was happening. He felt that it was good for his father and that lying there in the darkness did not matter so much. [Death, p. 252]

But within the space of a moment Andrew reverses field. He is now condemning Father Jackson and God and Christianity, and by implication Rufus' aunt and his mother.

They were standing at the edge of Fort Sanders and looking out across the waste of briers and of embanked clay, and Rufus was trying to hold his feelings intact. Everything had seemed so nearly all right, up to a minute ago, and now it was changed and confused. It was still all right, everything which had been, still was, he did not see how it could stop being, yet it was hard to

remember it clearly and to remember how he had felt and why it
had seemed all right, for since then his uncle had said so much.
[Death, *pp. 253–54*]

Hence the closing sentence of the novel—"But he did not ask, and
his uncle did not speak except to say, after a few minutes, 'It's
time to go home,' and all the way home they walked in silence"
(*Death*, p. 255)—is actually Rufus' response to the central paradox of the novel. The contentment Rufus experiences as he is
drawn into companionship with his uncle and which obliterates
his fear of death and fear for his father's loneliness is, in fact, an
illusion. Like the darkness which was first shelter then a monster,
the "accident of compassion" is also deceptive. The novel ends,
then, with Rufus "hovering over Cartesian vortices" as he tries to
hold his feelings intact.

iii

In an attempt to develop the natural lines of Rufus' awakened
moral sensitivity, in the spring of 1950 Agee wrote his novella
The Morning Watch. It concerns a young boy, Richard, a boarding student at a High Church Episcopal boys school in the Tennessee mountains. With his schoolmates Hobe and Jimmy, Richard participates in an all-night prayer vigil during the early morning hours of Good Friday in 1923. Instead of returning to the
dormitory immediately following their half-hour watch, however,
Richard first detains Hobe and Jimmy by an excessive act of
piety, watching the Blessed Sacrament for an additional half-
hour, then encourages them to run off to a Sand Cut to go
swimming. Agee's notes and letters indicate that he was still concerned about writing a story which would be more than autobiography. One entry, for instance, combines his plan for work with
questions similar to those he had asked himself in his letter to
Father Flye of November 1945.

What really am I after in this story, and is it worth doing?

Religion at its deepest intensity or clarity of childhood faith and emotions; plus beginnings of a skeptical intellect and set of senses; how the senses themselves, and sexuality, feed the skeptical or non-religious or esthetic intellect; efforts at self-discipline. Religious-esthetic-biological experiences carrying with them above all, religious experience of an unusually fine kind, and the innocent certainty that it is doomed. [19]

This note provides a good insight into the novella. For, as Victor Kramer has recently written, Richard's "desire to feel his faith, and how that desire is crushed by other influences, is the core to which all events of *The Morning Watch* are related." [20] Moreover, it is especially interesting in light of Agee's remarks on faith and religious consciousness prepared for a symposium entitled "Religion and The Intellectuals," sponsored by the *Partisan Review* and printed in February 1950 (17:10-13). Asked what had made "religion more credible than it formerly was to the modern mind," Agee answered:

I only suppose that in many the intellect, becoming less credulous of the power and claims of intellect even at its best, becomes more receptive to non-intellectual data.

Since the "validity" is super-rational, it cannot be rationally determined. . . .

Religious and rationalistic faith do differ in one crucial respect. The latter is belief in the supposedly credible and is open to question and change. The former requires belief in the incredible, in matters beyond the corroboration of reason or the senses.

The two statements which are essential premises of *The Morning Watch* are that religious faith is "super-rational," dependent to some extent on "non-intellectual data . . . beyond the corroboration of reason or the senses," and that "the senses themselves, and sexuality, feed the skeptical or non-religious or esthetic intellect." It is precisely the conflict between Richard's emotional response to religious images and discipline and his awakening intellect which creates the novel's significant ambiguity.

Agee's story is not wholly successful, however. As will be

shown, the concluding scene, when the boys go swimming, is
presented through an intricate network of symbols which even
Agee himself doubted. His incomplete draft notes indicate that he
feared that Richard's cherishing of a locust hull and killing of a
snake were too contrived, and that the story which led up to
them suffered from a lack of conviction.

> *To be done in terms of: the watching in the chapel; wanderings*
> *of the mind and efforts at prayer; memories of the dead father;*
> *imaginations of sex and sport; workings of guilt; excesses of reli-*
> *gious intention and complications of guilt and pride; the excite-*
> *ment of . . . dawn . . . the locust hull; . . . the snake. Is [the*
> *snake] too obvious a symbol, and the locust? They seem so.*
>
> *Is this worth doing? I can't get any solid hold of it or confi-*
> *dence in it.*
>
> *A much gentler way of seeing & writing it? Or more casual?*
> *Mine is very dry and very literary.*

Indeed, Richard's "excesses of religious intention" in the chapel
are always recognizable to the reader for what they are, and they
are often masterfully exploited for their humor. But there is a
sense that, as Agee is writing about his own boyhood, he is reach-
ing after effects. Much of the writing is vitiated by what Richard
Chase in a *Kenyon Review* article aptly calls an "overplus of
imagination." At times—for example, near the end of Part II—the
rhetoric is simply inflated by animism and aural effects, much
like his early poetry.

> *How about when they raise up the Cross with you on it and*
> *drop it deep into the hole they dug for it! And imagining that*
> *moment he felt a tearing spasm of anguish in the center of each*
> *palm and with an instant dazzling of amazed delight, remember-*
> *ing pictures of great saints, shouted within himself,* I've got the
> Wounds! *and even as he caught himself opening his palms and his*
> *eyes to peer and see if this were so he realized that once again this*
> *night, and even more blasphemously and absurdly than before, he*
> *had sinned in the proud imagination of his heart.* [MW, p. 107]

Richard's own inner voice is often less inflated than is the authorial voice. Always imagistic in his thinking, the character emphasizes the weight of the cross dropping with the alliteration of *d*'s and an exclamation mark. But the author speaks of "imagining . . . a tearing spasm of anguish." The sensation of physical pain—the words "tearing" and "spasm" in conflict—is as out of proportion to imagining as the overwrought image of "an instant dazzling of amazed delight" is consistent with it. And in the same context they are emotionally incongruent. With the remainder of the sentence including such words as "blasphemously," "absurdly," "sinned," "proud imagination," and "heart," there is ample support for Chase's criticism that the book is turgid with "a great surplus of poetical consciousness as compared with what the persons and situations of the story appear to necessitate; there is a disproportion between substance and form; between meaning and metaphor; and despite a great deal of local excitement and activity, there is a heavy inertness of the whole." [21]

This flaw is the first sign of a decline in Agee's postwar work— unless it simply supports Dwight Macdonald's contention that "Agee was seldom able to tell when he was hitting it and when he wasn't." [22] Nevertheless, *The Morning Watch* is important as one of Agee's artistic statements. Even the conclusion, which suffers most, leaves the reader with complex feelings regarding Richard's development. During his chapel hour Richard simply runs out of emotional gas: "No more I could do, he reflected, if I stayed all night. No more. No use: and he continued merely to look without thought at the emblazoned ruin" (*MW*, p. 119). Leaving the chapel with Hobe and Jimmy, realizing they are already late in returning to the dormitory and must face Father Whitman's punishment, Richard suggests that they play tennis. But this is considered too risky. Hobe suggests they go swimming in the Sand Cut. Steadily, as they walk by the hen house and the hog sty, passing the stile into the woods, Richard emerges from his religious frame of mind with its considerations of pride, mortal sin, and confession. While the others walk ahead, he stops to look at a locust shell. The exoskeleton, a natural memento mori, reminds him of pictures of prehistoric animals, geologic time spans, and figures of the Christian cosmology. Replacing the shell, he notices other skeletons—a "weathered oak tower," "relics of machinery," and "the dead cones of putty-colored sand" (*MW*, pp. 131–32). Within the context of these natural symbols Richard's swim, an obvious baptism, is intended to take on complex implications. Richard conceives of his swim as an act of physical mortification, an acceptance of the suffering of Christ; instead, it becomes an act of physical awareness so intense that Richard believes suicide might be an ultimate spiritual act, uniting the evolution of the earth and Christ's death on the cross:

> ... he was aware of the entire surface of his body as if it were fire, and every muscle seemed to feel its own exact shape and weight, and he wished that he need never come up and lay against the deepest trench of the bottom, his belly foundering in ooze, his eyes shut, staying his hands on rocks. [MW, pp. 135–36]

However, "even before he could command it ... his body was working for him," pushing him to the surface (*MW*, p. 137). Unfortunately for Richard, he never completely understands his mistake nor his body's response. *"Anyhow I tried,"* he says, "meaning at once that he had tried to stay down too long as an act of devotion and that he had tried to save himself from the deadliest of sins" (*MW*, p. 137). Of course the act is a perversion of his intention, and Agee tries to clarify it by another symbolic action, the killing of the snake.

Unlike the locust shell, which is only a skeleton, the snake is a beautiful physical presence, having just shed its old skin. In this satanic analogue, Richard "saw perfected before him, royally dangerous and to be adored and to be feared, all that is alien in nature and in beauty" (*MW*, p. 141). His first reaction, the effect of his natural baptism—"something new in him which he could not understand" (*MW*, p. 142)—is to protect the snake from Hobe's rock. But repulsed by the wounded snake, Richard suddenly picks up a rock and smashes its head, caring "only for one thing, to put as quick an end as he could to all this terrible, ruined, futile writing and unkillable defiance" (*MW*, pp. 143–44). Richard finally realizes that the snake, like Christ, is "unkillable defiance" and will not die until sundown. When Hobe at last casts the writhing body into the hog sty, Richard reflects that the snake "must be a way beyond really feeling anything, ever any more" (*MW*, p. 156). Thus the snake, which in the length of its suffering is related to the suffering Christ and in its rigor mortis is related in Richard's mind to his dead father, is beyond significance for him. Richard is left to walk into the dormitory to face Father Whitman's rules with only relics from his morning watch—a locust shell and a swollen hand from the slime of the snake.

This ending to *The Morning Watch* is related to an earlier story about Richard published in the *Harvard Advocate* in April 1930, "Boys will be Brutes" (116:29–33). Invading a nest of robins, Richard and another boy, Joe, are attacked by the mother bird. They succeed in killing all the nestlings but one before the mother chases them to the refuge of a wood where Richard vomits. The experience leaves both boys unchastened, however, and they depart for home with a lack of concern for what they have done. As in *The Morning Watch*, there is an implicit ambiguity. For while Richard and Joe initially detest killing at close quarters, they eventually take an excessive delight in it. While the experience is violent, it makes little impression on them,—also true of the closing scene in *The Morning Watch*. Agee's novella has been interpreted by John S, Phillipson as a Christian pageant of suffering and death and resurrection, the locust shell symbolizing suffering, the swim standing for death and rebirth, and the killing of the snake representing overcoming evil and death. [23] But Richard is not simply reborn by his swim. Rather, his physical excitation leads him to desire to take his own life, perverting his intention to suffer with Christ into an act of idolatry. His desire to protect the snake is not only the effect of his natural gentleness for animals, but also a result of this perverted rebirth. The snake is not only a symbol of Satan, but also Christ, both in his physical newness and in the length of his suffering, and of Richard's dead father. Thus, Richard is reborn, not to awareness (although the natural world assumes greater clarity in his eyes), but more explicitly, to an increased moral sensitivity which ironically prevents him from making clear distinctions between good and evil.

This moral ambiguity is hardly unique to Agee's vision. It must nevertheless be admitted that he had a poignant talent for expressing it. *The Morning Watch* and *A Death in the Family* reject the typical categories of American fiction by conceiving a world where redemption and love are found accidentally by unspoken needs rather than by conscious choice or desire. The detail of slime from the snake causing Richard's hand to swell is found in a similar incident in *A Death in the Family*, when Rufus is fascinated by ashes he finds beside his dead father's morris chair. Both Richard and Rufus wish to taste these substances. When Rufus does so, "his tongue tasted of darkness" (*Death,* p. 212)—the darkness of his father's death, which Andrew leaves forever disturbed. Richard does not taste the slime because Hobe is watching and because "he wanted the hand to clear gradually and naturally, the way the smudge clears from the forehead on Ash Wednesday" (*MW,* p. 145)—still a symbol of mortality. Thus, Agee's fictional protagonists are neither victims nor seekers. Nature does not bless them any more than human contact does. Rather, they redeem themselves by accidental gestures in response to some inner spirit. Ultimately they exploit an intense focus on what Agee once called the "battle ground on which [men] fight out [their] small personal epic between good and evil."

Agee's vision was never more deftly stated than in his last work of fiction, "A Mother's Tale," a short story written a year after *The Morning Watch* in November 1951, while he was recovering from his second heart attack. The story is an animal fable in which a mother cow tells her calves and their friends the story of a steer who has escaped the slaughterhouse. Throughout the long tale of the herding of the steers from the range, of shipping them in cattle cars to market, of the final fattening processes at the white-fenced stockyard, of the slaughter line and the chance, missed hammer stroke, and the torturous journey back to the range where The One Who Came Back tries to warn the remainder of the herd, the calves listening to their mother are similar to Rufus and Richard, full of questions they are unable to answer and ambitions they are unable to accomplish. At the crucial moment of the story—the description of the Man With the Hammer— the mother cow looks at her eager audience and questions her own senses: "This shining in their eyes: was it only excitement? no pity? no fear?" (p. 12). However, she is too inwardly horrified by the story to admit to the children that it is anything but a legend. The calves react predictably: her oldest son resolves to find out for himself, because "if she said a thing wasn't so, it probably was so. But you never could be sure." When the others have left, her youngest asks her poignantly, "What's a train?" (p. 18).

Implicit in "A Mother's Tale" is an ironic comment on the role of the story teller. Not only does the mother tell her children that the story is "just an old, old legend," but she is also living proof of the efficacy of the story-teller's art, a representative of the herd's rejection of the Prophet, The One Who Came Back. Because he had preached anarchy—"Each one is himself. . . . Not of the herd. . . . Obey nobody. Depend on none. . . . Break down the fences. . . . Never be taken. . . . Never be driven. Let those who can, kill Man. Let those who cannot, avoid him. . . . Kill the yearlings. . . . Kill the calves. . . . Bear no young" (pp. 16–17)—few accepted him. And in recalling The One Who Came Back, the mother cow realizes the paradox which had upset the Prophet's teaching: "Why, I am one alone. And of the herd, too. Both at once. All one" (p. 17). Hence the mother cow bears witness to the rejection of truth at the same time that her story telling is a tacit affirmation of its acceptance. Although she denies the Prophet, she continues to relate his story in the hopes that her children will accept it. Instead, each calf accepts it as he alone hears it. Thus the subtlety of Agee's touch is conveyed by the irony of his own role as fabulist. For like the mother of his tale, the narrator must realize that his story is the recreation of his own biases and that what will be heard will be the satisfaction of the biases of his audience. In its relation of the fragility of the mind's perceptions, "A Mother's Tale," then, is Agee's most refined statement on the nature of art and on the nature of truth.

On the whole Agee's fiction describes a progress consistent with his reaction to the horrors of the atomic age. His quest for an integrity by which he could survive his despair of "atomic liquefaction" was satisfied by responding to the memories of his own life. At the same time Agee came to realize that the past creates expectations which the present cannot hope to fulfill. Rufus in *A Death in the Family* finds the warmth of family companionship inadequate to answer the question of his father's death, and Richard in *The Morning Watch* finds the religious formulas of his training in conflict with his awakening emotions and intellect. Agee is not simply writing about the loss of innocence. In both books he touches on experiences and universal mysteries more profound than the identity crises which perplexed so many antiheroes in the fiction of the late 1940s and 1950s, especially in the work of J. D. Salinger, to whose creations Agee's characters are often compared. Perhaps for this reason alone it is unfortunate that Agee never finished *A Death in the Family*. In retrospect it appears that he was writing something more significant and enduring than the work of his contemporaries—a sensitive and comprehensive portrait of the human condition. Furthermore, publication of the finished story might have given him the conviction he so desperately lacked and needed.

Robert Fitzgerald has written that it is his belief that what Agee "was born to do, he did" ("Memoirs," p. 63). Though the statement is inevitably true, it is in the many ways that it is not true—that Agee left much of his best work unfinished and that what he spent his time finishing, especially the film scripts after 1949, did little to help him either personally or artistically—that Fitzgerald's statement is most revealing. Fitzgerald tells us that Agee had confessed to Helen Levitt shortly before he died that he had always felt that his true vocation was to be a poet but that he had found "it was too difficult" ("Memoir," p. 63). If Agee sincerely believed this—and there is no reason to suspect he did not—his evasion contains more significance than can ever be found in his verse. In this respect he did too much of what he was born to do, leaving readers thankful that he did some other things as well.

James Agee left *Time* magazine and discontinued his film column for the *The Nation* in the fall of 1948. He told friends that he was going to finish *A Death in the Family*, which he had begun the previous fall and which he worked at intermittently for at least two years more. He had already finished the commentary and dialogue for one film, *The Quiet One*, and had contracted with Huntington Hartford to write the screenplay for another, an adaptation of Stephen Crane's "The Blue Hotel." Also he had agreed to write an essay on silent film comedy for *Life* magazine. Although the death of his stepfather, Erskine Wright, in February 1949, slowed his work on the article, he went ahead and contracted for another *Life* essay on John Huston, which was published in September 1950, roughly at the same time that he finished the *Blue Hotel*. He sent in the script, received a critique toward the end of October, and left for Hollywood shortly thereafter to polish it and to begin work for Huston on his new film, *The African Queen*. It was while he was in California, working on the set all day, writing and drinking coffee most of the night and up at sunrise to play tennis with Huston, that he suffered his first heart attack in mid-January 1951.

Agee's coronary was only the physical aspect of this withering siege of activity. Although its other causes remain indistinct, it marked the end of most of Agee's original work. Within five weeks he was out of the hospital, and shortly thereafter he was back at work for Hartford on another Stephen Crane adaptation, "The Bride Comes to Yellow Sky." And in November he was back in the hospital. This time he took a somewhat more serious view of the matter, but not dangerously so. In a long letter he wrote to Father Flye at the time, he seems more stunned than frightened, wavering between boredom and depression. He was almost forty, "broke and unemployed with no job in sight." He had done little on the novel which he had left *Time* three years earlier to finish. He was buried in debts, run up by his heart attacks. He had a family, from whom he was separated, to care for. And he sensed he had little time to live because his life depended on "whether or not I can learn to be the kind of person I am not and have always detested; and because, knowing my own character pretty well, I know pretty well what my chances are, even though I will try." (*Letters*, pp. 194–95). Unfortunately he was correct. His life was submerged by a peculiar spiritual apathy which amounted to "caring much too little whether I live or die" (*Letters*, p. 189).

There is a complex and somewhat cruel similarity between Agee's ennui following this second heart attack and his consistent lack of deep conviction concerning his creative work and talent. It distinguishes him from other writers—Nathaniel West, F. Scott Fitzgerald, William Faulkner—who turned to Hollywood for hack work. Agee called it hack work, but for one reason or another—his love of the film, his need to commit himself totally to a given task, the simple enjoyment of being appreciated—his screen writing was both more and less to him than hack work. On the one hand he spoke of himself as a "creative" writer, an artist, and on the other he lamented that he was not doing his "own" work. He had already noted in his long draft of his review of *Monsieur Verdoux* that "the pressure of business is not merely pressure; it is an irresistibly strong attraction," [1] but he had not yet turned to fulfilling a request by *The New York Times* for an article on his feelings about writing screenplays, as opposed to reviewing them. Although he was incensed by the question, contending that it presumed his having been a "bully" as a critic and that he was therefore a "coward" as a writer, he went on to state that "the business of an artist is, evermore simply, to give the specific task all of the best in him which is appropriate to that task." [2]

If these passages suggest that Agee had grown content with the compromise he had dreaded ten years earlier—with commercial work as "an irresistibly strong attraction" and art as a task like any other—then it is a compromise sustained by the times in which he lived. In an extraordinary document, which appears to be an early postwar manifesto of principles for a proposed international political party, Agee had speculated on the kind of society which would permit an everlasting peace. His ideas are similar to the humble individualism on which he had based the tramp society of his Chaplin script, even to the extent that he foresaw the power of good turning into totalitarianism. Nevertheless, in the 1945–1948 period, he had believed a Third World War to be inevitable, and wrote "if war cannot be prevented, then it seems of the utmost importance that that side 'win' it . . . which retains any prospect whatever for the furtherance of the ideas we believe in." [3] This thought is in total contrast to Agee's statement to Father Flye in November 1951, following his second heart attack: "I think it extremely unimportant who 'wins' the next war" (*Letters*, p. 193). The difference in his attitude is significant, not because it indicates any declining interest in world affairs, but because it suggests a positive connection between the political-social environment of the twentieth century and Agee's creativity. Typically, the political and social crises of the time—the Depression, the prelude to and aftermath of the Second World War—coincided with his most productive periods. It is more than likely that the same holds true for most artists—that in times of crises they turn to their art as a stay against the chaos which threatens them. With Agee, the pattern is very clear—after *Let Us Now Praise Famous Men* he turned to criticism; after *A Death in the Family* and *The Morning Watch*, he turned to screen writing. These turns were not conscious; he admitted to Father Flye there was probably a connection he was failing to make between his lack of discipline and his ennui. But the pattern of his life is clearly in his art, and its meaning is difficult to avoid. The amorality of the reporter in "Dedication Day," the unrealizable regret of Irvine in "1928 Story," the ineffectual narrator in "Dream Sequence"—each of these characters is a reflection of Agee's sensitivity to one of the major themes of twentieth-century literature, the impotent spectator. Roberta Madden has already commented on Agee's treatment of Mr. Blanc in *The Blue Hotel*. But in defending Crane's "little silent man from the East" in the face of Agee's clearly defined, but at times heavy-handed, character, Mrs. Madden has not caught the drift of Agee's intention.[4] By having Blanc declare himself a journalist, Agee intended the audience to understand that, like Crane and himself, Blanc was a professional observer. What Agee wanted to emphasize was Crane's point to the fullest. In notes on Hartford's critique of his first draft he indicated the deeply personal irony with which he saw Blanc: "Crane shows him all through fight as more & more impersonal: later we learn why: he is the guiltiest man there: he saw the cheating & said nothing." [5]

It is important to realize that it was following this second heart attack, from the depths of a real despair that he had seen "the cheating & said nothing," that Agee wrote his last piece of fiction, "A Mother's Tale," with its sad, ironic comment on the permanence of art and the artist's effort. Perhaps the juxtaposition of the quality of this fiction and Mrs. Madden's misunderstanding despite a sensitive reading of Agee's script for *The Blue Hotel* is the only possible answer to the important and difficult question raised by Peter Ohlin: whether Agee's film work has "the same kind of finality and permanence of value as, for instance, *Let Us Now Praise Famous Men* and *A Death in the Family*" (Ohlin, p. 159). This question is evaded or avoided in all the full-length studies of Agee.[6] Ohlin himself dances around an answer, contending that films were not taken seriously in the 1950s and that scripts must be regarded as intentions, not as finished works of art. In the unpublished article for *The New York Times*, cited above, Agee himself alluded to this aspect of the work, hoping that critics would not blame him for what some other persons might have contributed to a given film. But this attitude is simply ironic. That a writer who had defined the central moral crisis of his time a failure of individual responsibility, specifically in reliance on group activities and collective guilt, should devote seven years of his life, and those the last seven, to a collaboration is, to repeat, simply ironic.

There is no way of equating the value and permanence of *Let*

Us Now Praise Famous Men and *A Death in the Family* and "A Mother's Tale" with Agee's screen writing. First of all, the ideas for the scripts did not begin with him. He was merely "called in" to visualize a story and to write or rewrite the dialogue. Secondly and most importantly, not he but the director or actor was responsible for the representation. It is nevertheless important to appreciate Agee's understanding of his screen writing. Certainly he did not consider the scripts merely as "intentions." In a letter of notes to director Fred Zinneman, he explained his working method.

I feel sure you will forgive me if as the writer I infringe on other territories, including those of the director: I can no more conceive of a writer's not trying to imagine the film as a whole, and finished, than of your not entering as deeply as you might wish to, into the writing stage of it.[7]

These are not the words of a scenarist, a composer of notes for a director. Agee thinks of the scripts as integral wholes—that is, as a kind of visually rendered novel. The term, however, is useful only insofar as it describes his craft. Despite the fact that Agee began his screen writing during the rebirth of independent productions, he was not creating a new genre. He was simply putting together a number of pieces, and he always kept in mind the picture it would form. But the visions he was reassembling belonged to Stephen Crane, Davis Grubb, C. S. Forester, and, as the endless hours of collaboration are taken into account, to John Huston, Charles Laughton, Bretaigne Windust, and countless others. Similarly, the means of representing these visions belonged to others. In all senses of the term Agee was a middleman, and his scripts belong to the same bastard state; they are neither film notes, means by which he could capture "the aesthetic reality in the actual world," nor novels, means by which he could verbally represent his own perceptions. So frustrated by this state of affairs is Kenneth Seib that he has argued that Agee's scripts are failures "because the visual image he sought was always subordinated to the verbal image he achieved" (Seib, p. 106). Roberta

Madden offers a similar comment on Agee's writing in *The Blue Hotel*. But these are more properly matters of feeling, not of fact. The certain accomplishment of Agee's screen plays can be found in what he wrote about them, such as the comment to Zinneman, and in the rough drafts themselves, a number of which fortunately survive and are collected in the University of Texas Library.

The ideal script for this purpose is that of *The African Queen*. Prior to writing for Huston, Agee had written a detailed analysis of his film work for *Life* magazine. As well, the rough drafts of the script indicate the precise point where Huston took over the writing after Agee's heart attack. For these two reasons the rough and finished drafts of *The African Queen* reveal some of Agee's goals and intentions as a script writer, as well as—to some extent—the compromises he made.

Contrary to popular opinion, he worked on a good deal of the script. As he noted in a letter to David Bradley, while discussing his original screenplay on the life of Gauguin, *Noa Noa:*

(African Queen, 1st draft, was 160 pages. The first hundred were mine and brought it through almost exactly half the story. The last 60, except a few scenes and interpolations, were Huston's; but the playing-time worked that his 60 an my 100 a-mounted to about the same.) [8]

Aside from its bibliographical worth, the statement has value as an interesting contrast to comments Agee had made about script writing, specifically for John Huston. In the *Life* article "Undirectable Director," he described the unique way Huston handled a script:

Most movies are like predigested food because they are mere reenactments of something that happened (if ever) back in the scripting stage. At the time of shooting the sense of the present is not strong, and such creative energy as may be on hand is used to give the event finish, in every sense of the word, rather than beginning and life. Huston's work has a unique tension and vitality because the maximum of all contributing creative energies converge at the one moment that counts most in a movie—the contin-

uing moment of committing the story to film. At his best, he makes the story tell itself, makes it seem to happen for the first and last time at the moment of recording. [Reviews, p. 336]

However, Agee's script for *The African Queen* lies at neither of these two extremes, nor between. It is clear that he adapted the C. S. Forester story in collaboration with Huston but that he wrote the script by visualizing the action—indeed, describing it down to the expressions on the actor's faces as though Huston were to have nothing more to do with it. Nor did Huston seem to mind, since he obviously had a deep respect for Agee.[9]

The novel is set in the Belgian Congo at the outbreak of the first World War.[10] Rose Sawyer, a Victorian spinster, is forced to join a rough-neck mail runner, Charlie Allnutt, in fleeing German troops who have burned her brother's mission outpost and caused his death. Basically Forester is concerned with Rose's sexual liberation through her confrontation with the elements—Allnutt being chief among these. At first she is dazed by her brother's death, submissive, "slow of speech and of decision." Vaguely, however, she wants to strike a blow for England. She finds her means gradually and begins to take advantage of Allnutt's cowardice, bullying him into making a voyage down the Ulanga and Bora rivers in a nearly sinking, low-beam excursion boat named the *African Queen*. Rose begins to believe it to be her heaven-sent mission to torpedo a German cruiser, the *Königin Luise,* which blocks English supplies on Lake Wittelsbach. Her relationship with Allnutt over the course of this treacherous journey evolves from a compassionate mother love to an eventual social necessity. Initially the cockney had been her means of bringing about God's vengeance on the Germans, as Forester puts it, a holy relic to a Joan of Arc. But when the *African Queen* sinks without fulfilling Rose's mission, "even her love for Allnutt seemed to be dead." It is only after their rescue, when an embarrassed British naval officer addresses Rose as "Mrs.—er—Miss" that her future with Charlie is sealed. Despite her "liberation," Rose is still plagued by guilt and the social consequences of having made love with Allnutt. She had righteously excused herself from any sin because of what she considered the divine blessing on her cause. But Rose's moral deference is not in any way equal to the mechanical limitations of the *African Queen,* and the novel ends on this ironic lack of resolution.

Agee apparently tried to retain Forester's Rose, but the part was simplified in revisions and significantly changed on the screen. Rose's sexual liberation is portrayed, among other places, in her lines spoken after her first experience with rapids: "I'd never dreamed that any—any mere—er—*physical* experience could be so—so *stimulating*" (*Scripts,* p. 197). Her ensuing moral problem was implied following a magnificent tropical rainstorm, freeing the *African Queen* from a morass of entrapping weeds. "God let us live," Rose says to Allnutt. "It wasn't for our sakes, either" (*Scripts,* p. 244). But these lines were cut from Huston's film. Forester's explicit theme of sin and vengeance was then wiped out by Huston's insertion of a scene in which Rose prays for deliverance. "Judge us not for our weakness but for our love," Miss Hepburn whispers. Thus the providential rainstorm approves rather than rebukes Rose for her role as Allnutt's natural wife. Forester's picture of Rose, with her frenetic fancies of patriotism and justification by works, undermined by a basically sensual nature, is simplified in Huston's treatment to a story of two people who fall in love and overcome common hardships.

The scripts exist in five separate briefs. Two, in Agee's hand, contain drafts in various stages of development, some of which were filmed, many others of which were deleted from the production schedule. There are also some scenes which appear very much as they were finally published in *Agee on Film: Five Film Scripts.* The remaining three briefs contain dated typescripts. Two of these contain Agee's work, while the third brief contains material written by both Huston and Agee. It is primarily material for which Agee had written rough notes, with completed dialogue for one scene. Shortly preceding the scene in which the *African Queen* is sighted by two German officers, the following note occurs in the typescript: "1-17-51. NOTE—from here on rough notes which J.A. had intended re-doing before typing."

Another note, at the conclusion of the Shona sequence, reads as follows: "1-18-51. Beg. J.H. Rough Draft." [11] This break provides an ideal point for comparison, for it juxtaposes two similar sequences—the rapids above Shona, written by Agee, and the rapids below, written by Huston; they reveal the distinct orientation of both artists, who possessed at the same time a remarkable similarity of approach.

For instance, in his script Agee writes interior monologues, physical descriptions, and characterizations of the action, as if he were writing a novel. Allnutt is described as "a little scared, knowing that Rose is a neophyte at steering and being a woman, may get rattled—but mainly he is feeling fine" (*Scripts*, p. 196). At the same time Rose's face is "extraordinarily chiseled and tense; her eyes are hard as diamonds." The characters' reaction to a buried rock is described as "scaring the daylights out of Allnutt and tightening Rose's face still more into this simulacrum of fear (he is comforted out of his own fears, seeing this face)" (*Scripts*, p. 196). The layers of Allnutt's emotions, the description of Rose's face, the complex interaction between the two characters, are the result of an imaginative process almost too refined to be helpful to either a director or an actor. Huston's writing, on the other hand, is equal only to his purpose. There is sparse indication of action and gesture. The metaphors are either borrowed from or suggested by Forester's writing. Rushing through the cataract below Shona, "*The African Queen* bucks like a bronco. The air is full of spray and of the ROAR of rushing water." Rose "rides the mad tide like a Valkyrie." And exchanges between the characters are indicated only by camera shots:

FULL SHOT—THE AFRICAN QUEEN
plunging down a narrow ribbon of water between vertical faces of rock.

CLOSE SHOT—ALLNUTT
as he waves at the engine and shouts something that is drowned out by the ROAR of the waters.

CLOSE UP–ROSE

She shakes her head and her lips form the words: "I can't hear."

CLOSE SHOT–ALLNUTT gesticulating frantically. He moves forward into a CLOSE UP and shouts:

ALLNUTT *(shouting)* Need fuel! We got to get fuel!

CLOSE SHOT–ROSE

She nods, to show her understanding of their plight.

FULL SHOT–THE AFRICAN QUEEN [Scripts, *p. 218*]

By the comparison it is apparent that Agee's film writing has similarities to his film criticism. Dwight Macdonald, among others, has commented on his "directorial imagination which sometimes remade the movie inside his head as he watched it, so that what came out on his page was often more exciting than what had appeared on the screen." [12] In the same way, in writing a script he used another's conception as a springboard for creating his own. Obviously, however, this process avoided the major responsibility of an artist, his obligation to represent his own ideas and emotions. In writing criticism and adaptations, Agee was not concerned with the whole range of aesthetic problems which had plagued his creative work. On the other hand, these activities permitted him to be a moralist and to think of himself as a writer. Though it is not known whether Agee was aware of this evasion in his work, the tactic is strongly suggested by his involvement in the collaborative effort of script writing. The dichotomy between his conception of himself as an artist and his recognition of his failure to do his "own" work resulted in a demonstrable situation in which he continued to practice a craft even as a marked decline in the quality of his own conceptions set in.

Attention to Agee's two early commercial scripts, *The Blue Hotel* and *The African Queen,* reveals his real talent as a writer accommodating itself grudgingly to another way of seeing. His frequent use of the first-person plural, "We detail or bring into salience," is a novelist's point of view: that of the observer watching and selecting relevant material. It differs essentially from Huston's, where the mind's eye and the camera are one, attentive to making rather than seeing the moment of action. Yet there are similarities of approach, which reveal the ways movie-making influenced his writing. Agee's and Huston's common reliance upon the close, medium, and long stationary shots is an effort to place the camera in such a position that the action tells the story. It was also a way to objectify a scene, so that attention could be paid to more subjective details. There is therefore very little dollying, few severe angles, and minimal zoom shooting in both *The Blue Hotel* and *The African Queen*. Agee showed his special awareness of Huston's camera work when he noted the problems in filming *Key Largo*:

> *Most of the action in* Key Largo *takes place inside a small Florida hotel. The problems are to convey heat, suspense, enclosedness, the illusion of some eighteen hours of continuous action in two hour's playing time, with only one time lapse. The lighting is stickily fungoid. The camera is sneakily "personal"; working close and in almost continuous motion, it enlarges the ambiguous suspensefulness of almost every human move. . . .*
>
> *Much that is best in Huston's work comes of his sense what is natural to the eye and his delicate, simple feeling for space relationships: his camera huddles close to those who huddle to talk, leans back a proportionate distance, relaxing, if they talk casually.* [Reviews, pp. 327–28]

Appropriately, he tried to make use of the observation in the camera work for his television adaptation of *The Blue Hotel*, a job Huston seems to have arranged and consulted on. Although the moving camera is somewhat more necessary to interior locations, Agee, like Huston, did not want it to intrude upon the action. Rather, he relied on close-ups, one portrait after another, to reveal the minute gestures and nuances of the action and reaction between characters.

One of the best examples of the objectively close yet subjectively moving camera is found in a card game and fight sequence in *The Blue Hotel*. The Swede's proposition for a second game of high five is made in a medium shot. The camera moves in during the Swede's debate with Scully, but only to medium close, focusing on the Swede's face from the innkeeper's angle. As the other characters are polled, the camera is in close for each of their lines. When they move to the table as a group, the camera pulls back to include them all. The game begins with close-ups until a monotony and rhythm, mimicking the deal, is established. Then the camera begins to circle, moving into essential action and finally into a close-up of the Swede at a critical moment. But to establish a perspective on this action, Agee inserts a medium-close shot of Scully reading a newspaper across the room. The sounds of the game are brought up in the background as the camera moves in on Scully. When the Swede suddenly accuses Johnnie of cheating, the focus is quickly cut to a long shot, which paralyzes the action for two seconds. Then the camera cuts close on each speaker, editing with the rhythm of the argument until immediately before its climax, when it begins to circle again. "As the CAMERA thus ropes them in they all close tighter and tighter against one center as if it were literally a rope around them: they come as close as five people can get" (*Scripts*, p. 440). Although the camera in this sequence has in a sense interpreted the action by "roping" the characters, it has allowed for the device by the very careful creation of tension through close-up portraits (which, for the most part, follow the play of the cards around the table) framed by medium and long shots. Thus, as the camera eye moves, it does not intrude upon the action but acts out of a logical response to it.

Other areas in which Agee's aesthetic instincts paralleled Huston's were also outlined in the *Life* article. Agee claimed that Huston's range was "surprisingly narrow, both in subject matter and technique." He found him "leery of emotion—of the 'feminine' aspects of art." Secondly, he felt his use of sound and dialogue wanting. "He has not shown much interest in exploring the tremendous possibilities of the former or in solving the crippling problems of the latter." In comparison to Eisenstein, Agee found Huston's editing was "distinctly unadventurous" (*Reviews*,

p. 330)—but in fact, Huston's films were edited by the studio. Agee, on the other hand, had always been attentive to sound and editing, and his work for Huston shows a close relationship to his previous experiments. If his attempt to adapt the full range of Rose Sawyer's character in *The African Queen* was to introduce "feminine" aspects into Huston's work, Agee had little chance for it in *The Blue Hotel,* which at the time was typical Huston material of men under pressure. However, Agee's notes for the sound in that picture, especially in the magnificent opening sequence, are reminiscent of the best uses of sound and silence throughout his work: the opening of "The House," the entirety of "Man's Fate," the closing "On the Porch" essay from *Let Us Now Praise Famous Men,* and the mixture of street noises and interior silences in *The Quiet One.* The film opens as follows:

TITLE
on black screen above center:

NEAR THE MIDDLE OF THE UNITED STATES
O.s., quiet, but swiftly louder, the humming, then hammering of rails; then over this, increasing SOUND, the SOUND of a hoarse, old-fashioned train whistle coming swiftly nearer: two long blasts, one short, one long, which trails down and out.

Over the fading train whistle and increasing train
SOUND

FADE IN

TITLE

below center:

TOWARDS THE END OF THE NINETEENTH CENTURY
Start the rapid SOUND of a train bell, SWOOP SOUND of bell
and train up suddenly two seconds before
                              CUTTING TO

CLOSE SHOT—A TRAIN (NITE)
Instantly bring SOUNDS of train and bell up as loud as the audi-

ence can stand. A transcontinental express-train crosses through r.s. to l.s. at frightening velocity. CAMERA is pulling back from a close shot at medium height of the train. In the train's wake, a long luminous ruche of snow is raised, filling the screen, and slowly sinking, as SOUNDS dwindle o.s. [Scripts, pp. 393–94]

178
The Full
Life is Full
of Crap

Agee's explicit intentions for the scene are revealed in his reaction to a critique of the sequence. In analyzing Agee's first draft, a Hartford associate, G. W. Tobin wrote:

Eliminate all shots of train—use sound of train over titles and dark screen and over light changes in first scene, to denote train off stage. This would speed, and concentrate opening. [13]

Horrified at a dissociation of sound and image, Agee wrote this lengthy explanation and defense in his notes:

Train shot done close-to, & pulling away, wd cost a maximum 15 seconds. [It creates?]: 1) powerful opening image, visual & sounds; 2) velocity of visible train greatly intensifies loneliness of town, [largeness?] of land, & . . . silence; 3) The synchronisations of the falling wake of snow dust, the falling [sound?] and the utmost pull back of camera, "raises a curtain" and cocks the trigger for the story.

Sound alone can impart none of this; if used, it should under no circumstances be used over the light changes; they get their best power from silence.

Agee's work on editing shows a similar effort to integrate a number of elements without losing their individuality. In writing notes for the Shona and Ulanga falls sequences of *The African Queen* Agee indicated that he wanted to create the illusion of one unbroken shot of danger after danger. The effect would be to take the audience down the rapids, so that Charlie's and Rose's efforts would be their only means of escape. It would be the same effect, he noted for Huston, "as Audie runs-away *for* the audience in *Red Badge.* [14] More comprehensive notes on editing are found in the rough draft of Agee's 1953 original screenplay on the life of Gauguin, *Noa Noa.* [15] His attention to the relation-

ship of editing rhythm to camera angles, sounds, and lighting in
Gauguin's and Van Gogh's early-morning walk through the streets
of Arles indicates an increasing confidence in cinematic techniques:

> *This is an essentially speechless but very happy walk, with a
> crescendo of happiness expressed in change of light and color, for
> we are walking through the rising of the sun. We shift from the
> blue-green, then green blues, of the foregoing scene, never show-
> ing the sun, but always its effects, through the reds, to the yel-
> lows, to the yellow-silver, as the dominant casts of our shots;
> meanwhile, without music (if it can carry thus), we hear only the
> awakening of a pastoral town and the crisp heelbeats of the two
> friends. Meanwhile, too, the town is awakening. Windows being
> pushed open. Bedding thrust out for air. Slops emptied. The first
> few people emerging. Wild, glad cries of roosters and babies.
> Scolding of mothers and wives, ad lib. A very young lover pro-
> ceeding home, sober, but high as a kite. A recognizable equivalent
> of the postman Rollins, whom Vincent painted. Vincent is silent
> with joy and with pride in his imposing friend; he salutes these
> people by pantomime rather than voice (beyond adlib); a few
> look after the two; most don't. Build as high as possible, through
> change of light and color, and through sound; and through pull-
> shots and more static shooting and cutting, as best turn out to
> befit the terrain and the practical possibilities. The mood is one
> which starts with crisp euphoria and steadily heightens, and must
> kick off a still higher mood. (NOTE: If pull-shots can be used,
> keep them slow, and let the two keep catching up and walking
> past Camera, cutting as they do. Ideally, however else done, this
> should be a cutting sequence, rather than one filled with dis-
> solves; and if it works well enough, should be done without any
> musical assistence.) [p. 9]*

In creating this "crescendo of happiness"—which in this scene,
incidentally, is more Van Gogh's than Gauguin's—Agee makes
careful use of color, sound, camera positions, and rhythms. The
colors move through a consistently intensifying spectrum: blue-

green, green-blue, reds, yellows, and yellow-silver. The sounds begin with "crisp heelbeats" and "windows being pushed open." Then there are "slops emptied" and roosters crying, babies and human voices. The camera pulls away, as though carried by a news photographer retreating before an important personage, and is overtaken. It should be noted that this unabashedly subjective camera is distinctive of *Noa Noa* and of Agee's later films. In effect, it is an attempt to exert a greater influence over the material. In another note on *Noa Noa*, concerning the filming of Gauguin's impression of Van Gogh's room, Agee illustrates the full-blown complexity of this technique:

> ... we must always be able to carry our own perception, and Gauguin's figure and reactions, in balance.... Throughout this passage, we use the Camera in a winding, flicking, prowling, continuous dance, full of lift and gaiety in the wheeling and cutting and reverse angles and in the contrasting faces and gaits and reactions to things seen and lines spoken. [p. 10]

This subjectivity is like that he uses in *A Death in the Family*. He wants the "winding, flicking, prowling" eye of the camera to be Gauguin's eye. However, the room and the furniture, represented by slightly distorted dimensions in the set and filter on the camera, suggests Van Gogh's paintings of his room. The "balance" Agee declares so essential, then, is between these two subjective viewpoints, which compose the scene.

There is a question, however, as to how much subjectivity a film can represent. Unlike a novel—where Agee could indicate a change in point of view by a paragraph or by identification of a speaker, where he could separate dialogue and interior monologue by punctuation—a film unrolls a fairly simple relationship between subject and object. It represents the conscious, the unconscious, or the subconscious power of sight and, to some extent, of hearing. Hence it is difficult to give the camera eye so much subjectivity, because it has only limited, and very explicit, means of expressing it. The natural recourse in film is to drama, the interaction between characters, relying, of course, on actors for its representation. But what Agee, under the influence of F. W. Murnau's experiments in "The Last Laugh", had begun to do in "The House"—to use the camera eye as his own consciousness—he continued to do in his later commercial films, especially in *Noa Noa* and *Tanglewood Story*. The effect of this technique is to emphasize the relationship between the artist and his story, rather than the relationships inherent in the story itself. The most obvious example of this problem is Agee's attempt to equate the camera eye with the eye of God, recalling the dilemma expressed in his Exeter poem, "Pygmalion," where the creator crushes his creation in an act of zealous love. This deification of the camera eye, which can be found specifically in *The African Queen* and *Tanglewood Story*, is one indication of Agee's declining artistry. For it points to his decreasing ability to represent the objects of his consciousness and his increasing need simply to express his response. As in "Pygmalion," the creator who destroys his creation in an outburst of "love" does so for two reasons: because he cannot see his creation for what it is and therefore respect it, and/or because he cannot respect his own ability to create.

Planning the filming of the rainstorm which frees the *African Queen* from its morass in the delta reeds, Agee indicates in the script that the camera moves across the sky and mountains—the sound track "held way down ... as if heard in a dream or in imagination" (*Scripts,* p. 239)—to the places of Rose and Charlie's struggles: the river, the mission clearing, the bluffs at Shona, the rapids, the waterfall beneath which they made love, the delta itself, which in the rainfall is rising slowly "with a new kind of energy" (*Scripts,* p. 241). In notes to his draft, however, he explains the significance of the shot:

Object is to use rain & river in a sort of ... hyperbole to bring leverage in under the lifting & drifting & falling that which now pick up—as if the whole of this part of a [cataract?], & sky are, as it were, collaborating, thanks to Rose's "Providence", for one purpose—to get the African Queen *on the Lake .... The essence of it is "liberation through Providence in the peace of God"; one strong analogy is a particular kind of dying ... the benificence &*

tenderness of a death bestower after living too long & suffering too much—and I think there should be this kind of stillness, breathlessness & tenderness in these shots.

On film this "collaboration" between earth and sky is enhanced by montage. The camera, however, becomes the "death bestower," bringing "stillness, breathlessness & tenderness" to Rose and Charlie.

In the notes on *Tanglewood Story* Agee specifically speaks of the camera as "The Eye of God." [16] The result of a collaboration with Howard Taubman, then music critic for *The New York Times,* this film is a story of five or six young musicians who study for the summer at the Boston Symphony's Tanglewood Festival. Excepting several fine scenes, it is one of Agee's few really poor works. "At its dead center," he explained in his long letter to director Fred Zinneman,

the film is simply about an art and a vocation: about music, and musicians. . . . I cannot imagine a more deeply moving or heartening film: for it is a film about the human spirit, or soul, and about the courage, and grace-of-God (i.e., talent or genius) which must combine to serve the human soul, and the sense of the super-human soul. . . . In a sense . . . this is, in fact a religious film. [pp. 1–2]

Clearly, if such were its core, *Tanglewood Story* might have been all that Agee anticipated, for it combined the theme he felt central to his own life: the dedication of the spirit to a work of art. The drafts illustrate, however, that he was simply overwhelmed by the possibilities. The characters emerge as stereotypes. Their vocations and their interrelations are given superficial treatment, and the result is a lack of focus, a dissipation of an overly complex plot into a number of trivial incidents. Agee only complicates these problems by attempting to rescue the conventionality, which he suspected, by the music. The finale is a good example. In the first drafts, the picture was to close on a performance of a piano concerto, either Beethoven's Fourth or Fifth, in which the two main characters would work out the difficulties of their love affair against the musical score, realizing in the end that they must serve their art before one another. But in the final draft they come to this realization in a parked car. Agee then dissolves to the Music Shed for the final Tanglewood concert of the season, a performance of Beethoven's Ninth Symphony. In the same letter to Zinneman he writes the purpose is:

. . . to tie up the whole picture and lift it beyond anywhere it has been, through music at its ultimate, perfectly performed: and, through this music at the right moments, to see our players for the last time, hearing the music and in reaction to it; and to bind the music and these individuals and their stories on through, to a sense of what music means to the human race. [p.27]

Given this premise, it is easy to see how *Tanglewood Story,* had it been filmed, would have failed. Agee invests persons and events with a significance the story does not earn for them. The real cause of this treatment is suggested by comparing Agee's notes with a remark he once made in his film criticism. He had told director Zinneman that he would feel bound "even more by love and interest than as a script writer, to indicate at least my own ideas, bar by bar, of what is going on among the performers and listeners, and how to shoot [the finale]." [17] His concern is reminiscent of the comment he had made when reviewing *Since You Went Away:* "When the consciousness blurs into love, it means fidelity to dream." In a word, Agee's impulses for *Tanglewood Story* are a lapse into the worst kind of romanticism, a magnification of his feeling and responding self until it blurs the objects of his consciousness. It is precisely this kind of lapse which demonstrates the decline in his artistry. Once the tension between the mystical and the mundane, sprung at the heart of his creativity, was lost, he became merely another sensitive and sentimental young man. Here it is important to recognize the truth of Robert Fitzgerald's observation that "Jim's weakness and strength were not so easy to tell apart" ("Memoir," p. 61). Many of Agee's notes for *Tanglewood Story* recall passages from *Famous Men.* He wrote Zinneman that the film requires the "most unassuming and unaffected kind of camera . . . for the kind of naturalism so well perceived and brought into context that it is raised into the level of poetry" (pp. 33–34). In his final story outline before writing dialogue, however, he had indicated that the camera work of the finale was "to serve and reveal the music . . . . as if it were 'The Eye of God,' perceiving with impartial intimacy and impersonal tenderness, the General . . . crowd (pp. 96–97). Perhaps the phrasing of this last note reveals the kind of disintegration taking place in his work. For it presumes that a work of art—the music in its relation to the conflicts of the characters, the film in its relation to the conflicts of its audience, are restorative. Although Agee harbored this feeling throughout his life, his finest creations are the result of his struggle against it; when his representations were fine, they were, as he noted of John Huston's *San Pietro,* "clear of urging or comment." But the weakness with which he was clutching at these extremes toward the end of his life can be seen in his tenuous yoking of "impartial" with "intimacy," "impersonal" with "tenderness," as if the words themselves could temper the dichotomy.

A further indication of decline is Agee's inclusion in his film scripts of previously used literary devices. Among others, there is the Virgilian image of a wheeling starry sky, which he had used throughout "Anne Garner" and which closes *The Blue Hotel* and opens the five-part series "Mr. Lincoln" for the television *Omnibus.* The opening sequence of the *Omnibus* series, in fact, borrows heavily on the dialogue, setting, and images of "Anne Garner."[18] The most significant reuse of literary material, however, is Richard's swim from *The Morning Watch,* which Agee makes into a major scene in *Noa Noa.* Agee began this film biography of Gauguin shortly after finishing the *Omnibus* series in the early spring of 1953. According to Whittaker Chambers, his former officemate at *Time,* Agee was obviously a dying man. He took short, painful steps, and his shoulders stooped slightly.[19] He was again drinking heavily and suffering from insomnia. In this state he borrowed his uncle's South Pacific diaries and began to make a film out of Gauguin's notebook of his life in Tahiti. Obviously he had great sympathy for Gauguin, who had sacrificed everything—his family, friends, life in France—for his art. But the sympathy was also self-serving. Agee begins the film by "blessing" Gauguin's corpse, moving the camera in the sign of the cross over the body. Having consecrated his subject and made the obvious analogy between his suffering and the suffering of Christ, he borrows the crucial scene of the picture from the climax of *The Morning Watch.*

Gauguin has returned to France from Tahiti for the first time. It is the eve of his Paris exhibit, and he is explaining to assembled friends his freedom from jealousy over the supposed infidelity of his vahine Tehura. Asked if he will return to Tahiti, Gauguin replies, "I have no plans whatever." There ensues an argument over the predicted success or failure of the exhibit. Gauguin makes it clear that he is no patient idealist; he would revel in vengeance over Paris' philistines if they considered his show a success. A friend warns him, "Don't forget: Your show may fail."

WE PAN ALONG TO GAUGUIN, INTO CLOSEUP. Pause.

*GAUGUIN (hateful, irony) You think so? (with
burning bitter arrogance) We'll see.*

DISSOLVE

*PANNING SHOT—MUSIC UNDER
(a light-scored conflicting of French and Tahitian motifs.)*

*We PAN ACROSS a corner of the dark studio, and past a window
to a couch where Gauguin lies asleep. En route we glimpse his
ratty luggage, some Tahitian curios, and through a window, the
sleeping glow of Paris. We DOLLY IN on Gauguin whose dream-
ing face works a little; then a*

SLOW, WELTERING DISSOLVE

*CLOSE DOWNSHOT—THE SURFACE OF CALM SEA WATER
Music throughout. To be shot in tank and lagoon. . . .*

*Gauguin stands, proud and uneasy, in a Tahitian canoe. The
Canoe-Master (from fishing sequence) tells him: "You may dive*

only once." Looking about him, Gauguin meets the eyes of others in the canoe: fine native types; then Mette, Aline, Vincent. All, looking at him, politely doubt his competence. With an air of bravely facing the ultimate he draws a deep breath and dives.

We follow him down to a sea floor so deep it is semidark in crystal water, and among the strange and marvelously colored sea-plants and corals he searches out shell-fish, for their pearls. He opens the first two with a knife and puts the pearls in his mouth. Thenceforth he is too short of breath to open the shells; he just cuts them loose and tucks them into his pareu—*which he wears almost as a G-string. Suffering for air, he sights still more shells. We intensify to maximum the conflict between lack of air, exertion, and greed for more pearls. Carrying all the shells he can in each hand, plus his knife, and half asphyxiated, he stands upright, settles his feet against knife-edged coral, and with all his strength springs upward, his cut feet trailing blood. We milk the ascent for maximal suffering and will-he-make-it, especially during the last few feet. Our last shot plunges upward rapidly from below-surface and as camera bursts through we*

CUT TO

INT.—THE DURAND-RUEL GALLERY—PARIS—DAY—PAN AND TRACK SHOT—GALLERY GOERS [Scripts, pp. 95–96]

The conflict of Gauguin's dream—whether to gather pearls or to surface—is tantamount to that in Richard's swim: whether to suffer with Christ to become sanctified or to live with his new-found powers. And as he had written explicitly in *The Morning Watch*, Agee urged David Bradley that they emphasize Gauguin's "effort to hold himself down to the bottom." [20] Thus in both scenes Agee's intention is to portray the desire for sanctification, or the beautiful as self-destructive. Furthermore, both plunges are made under the fear of sexual threat, Richard's after he has noticed the difference between his penis and Hobe's and Jimmy's, Gauguin's in recollection of Tehura's supposed infidelity. There emerge from this comparison, then, three distinct threats affecting Agee's two characters: a threat to sexual identity or to creativity in general; a threat to accomplishment, either in sanctity or artistry; and a threat to life, which is subliminal in the previous two.

Obviously these threats are interrelated and have personal significance to Agee himself. The threat of death permeates everything he writes. Perhaps its representation is not always so specific as a remembrance of the death of his father, but there are consistent reverberations of the significance of that death. For the most part Agee's treatment of the theme of death falls within the American Romantic tradition, which sees death as the ultimate sensual-sexual experience. This is as true of "Anne Garner" and the wedding pair of the "Epithalamium" as it is of Richard and Gauguin. However, by avoiding a final acceptance of the tradition in the resurrection myth, Agee's characters do not reflect any greater awareness of life but rather a heightened consciousness of culpability and mortality. It is this theme which is expressed in the "homelessness" of Richard and Rufus as well as of Agee himself in *Let Us Now Praise Famous Men.* And for this reason the endings of *Noa Noa* and *Tanglewood Story* do not ring true. In a long speech to his weak-willed friend Vernier, Gauguin speaks of the constant stripping away of all he had loved—his friends, his family, his possessions, his eyesight, and finally his art. The prospect is bleak. "The real effort," he says, "has always been, simply, to be true to my own soul. And that I have been and now I know the price "(*Scripts,* p. 139). Yet close to death Gauguin mutters Lear's words to Cordelia, "Come let's away to prison," as Agee notes, "with their strange appositeness to him, Vincent, and all artists" (*Scripts,* p. 134). This redemption through suffering the artistic vocation is strange to Agee's work. Yet its very strangeness is no cause for rejecting it. It is its exaggeration which renders it artistically suspect and which, when coupled with the clear fact of Agee's life, that he was dying with the conviction he had failed to become a great artist, gives it undeniable significance. Agee's earliest and only desire was to be an artist. At the same time his art had to serve the cause of his salvation. Although he was led to believe—because of the Romantic tradition of the artist and especially because of Joyce's conception of the role—that art was amoral, the real accomplishment of his work was the tension he sustained between a record of his perceptions or conceivings and his evaluation of them. When that tension was loosened, when he failed to sustain that balance between record and response which he realized as absolutely essential to the task, his art degenerated into sentimentality and bathos. Although it is impossible to say what could have happened if he had lived, it is quite evident in the notes for *Noa Noa* and *Tanglewood Story,* as well as in Agee's letters to Father Flye about his Williamsburg project, that he was losing his grip. Whether this was the result of his numerous heart attacks, the terrible psychic torment he endured, his indefatigable concern for others, or a simple loss of will to live is not known. In any case, in certain moments he was able to understand his general deceleration with equanimity. "At moments," he wrote Father Flye a month before his death, "I wonder whether those who go, as I do, for a Full Life, don't get their exact reward, which is that the Full Life is full of crap." Then he added philosophically: "At other moments I realize equally well, that this is what Life is all about" (*Letters,* pp. 227–28).

In preparing this edition, I have tried to keep the notes to an absolute minimum without sacrificing scholarship. Insofar as the following works are cited throughout the text, bibliographical information and abbreviations are included here. Quotations from these works are followed by the abbreviated title and page number in parenthesis.

Reviews   Agee, James R. *Agee on Film: Reviews and Comments,* ed. David Manning White, New York, 1958; Boston, 1964.

Scripts   ————— *Agee on Film: Five Film Scripts,* ed. David Manning White, New York, 1958, Boston, 1964.

Prose   ————— *The Collected Short Prose of James Agee,* ed. Robert Fitzgerald, Boston, 1969; New York, 1970.

Poems   ————— *The Collected Poems of James Agee,* ed. Robert Fitzgerald, Boston, 1969; New Haven, Conn. 1969.

Death   ————— *A Death in the Family.* New York, 1957; 1963.

"DD"   ————— "Dedication Day. Rough Sketch for a Moving picture," *Politics* 3 (April 1946):121-25.

"House"   ————— *"The House:* Notes for a Moving Picture," *New Letters in America* 1, ed. Horace Gregory, New York, 1937, 37-55.

Letters   ————— *The Letters of James Agee to Father Flye.* New York, 1962.

FM   ————— *Let Us Now Praise Famous Men.* Boston, 1941; 1960.

MW   ————— *The Morning Watch,* Boston, 1950; New York 1966.

"MT" _____ "A Mother's Tale," *The Best American Short Stories 1953*, ed. Martha Foley, Boston, 1953.

PMV _____ *Permit Me Voyage*. New Haven, Conn., 1934; 1935.

Behar Behar, Jack. "James Agee: The World of His Work," unpublished doctoral dissertation. The Ohio State University, 1964.

Concannon Concannon, Sister Jeanne M. "The Poetry and Fiction of James Agee: A Critical Analysis," unpublished doctoral disseration. The University of Minnesota, 1968.

"Memoir" Fitzgerald, Robert. "Memoir," in *Prose,* pp. 3–66.

Kramer Kramer, Victor A. "Agee: A Study of The Poetry, Prose and Unpublished Manuscript," unpublished doctoral dissertation. The University of Texas, 1966.

Mayo Mayo, Charles. "James Agee: His Literary Life and Work," unpublished doctoral dissertation. George Peabody College for Teachers, 1969.

Ohlin Ohlin, Peter. *Agee*. New York, 1966.

Perry Perry, J. Douglas. "James Agee and The American Romantic Tradition," unpublished doctoral dissertation. Temple University, 1968.

Seib Seib, Kenneth. *James Agee: Promise and Fulfillment*. Pittsburgh, 1968.

Synder Synder, John J. "James Agee: A Study of His Film Criticism," unpublished doctoral dissertation. St. John's University, 1969.

Essential to this study was the availability of a substantial collection of Agee manuscripts at the University of Texas. For an indication of its extent, the reader is directed to Victor Kramer's "James Agee Papers at the University of Texas," *University of Texas Library Chronicle* 8, no. 2(1967): 33–36. In general. I have followed the citation system used in the Manuscript Collection card catalogue, but in some cases I have emended the capitalization of titles. The Library, for instance, brackets all manuscript titles and dates not specifically identified in the manuscript, capitalizing only the first word of the title and the general category: "[Let us now praise famous men:Notes] ". I have retained the brackets but capitalized the titles. Where Library titles or dates are incorrect or vague, I have corrected them, yet retained the brackets in deference to absolute identification. Most of the manuscripts are not numbered; it is therefore impossible to cite page numbers except in the case of several letters or carbon typescripts. All the manuscripts verify that Agee was indeed a painstaking writer. He worked and reworked sentences, searching for the perfect rhythm and placement of phrases. I note this fact, because many of the manuscripts are categorized "incomplete" only because they are so extensively revised. Agee seldom changed the initial concept with which he sat down to write, but his drafts indicate that he worked long hours at his craft, assiduously earning his reputation as a stylist. At the same time, his spelling and punctuation were often erratic if not incorrect. I have standardized the spelling but let the punctuation stand. The one remaining problem is his handwriting. Anyone who has perused Agee's script will admit the difficulty of reading it. I have tried to the best of my ability to transcribe it accurately, to guess intelligently, and where the exigencies of soft lead and calligraphy conspire, to bracket either the best guess with a question mark or simply the word "illegible." Essential, too, were the letters of James Agee to Dwight Macdonald, kindly loaned to me by Mr. Macdonald. They cover the years 1927–1945, concentrated mainly during the 1930s. For the most part, I followed the same procedures in quoting from them as I did from the Texas material, standardizing spelling, allowing punctuation to stand as is, and bracketing dates not specifically noted on the holograph.

Preface

1. Sources and authors are: Richard Oulahan, "A Cult Grew Around a Many-Sided Writer," *Life* 55(November 1, 1963): 69–72; T. S. Matthews, "James Agee–'Strange and Wonderful,' " *Saturday Review* 49(April 16, 1966): 22–23; Dwight Macdonald, "Jim Agee, A Memoir," in *Against the American Grain* (New York, 1962), pp. 160–66; Alfred Kazin, "Goodbye to James Agee," in *Contemporaries* (Boston, 1962), pp. 185–87; Anonymous, "Tender Realist," *Time* 70 (November 18, 1957): 118; and F. W. Dupee, "Memories of James Agee," in *The King of Cats and Other Remarks on Writers and Writing* (New York, 1965), pp. 80–84. The quotations are taken from Dupee, p. 81, Matthews, p. 22, Macdonald, p. 164, and David McDowell in Oulahan, p. 72, respectively. The last two remarks are Dwight Macdonald's in "James Agee," in *American Grain,* p. 153, and W. M. Frohock in "James Agee–The Question of Wasted Talent," in *The Novel of Violence in America* (Dallas, 1957), p. 212.

2. "No Use Talking," *The New Republic* 147(August 13, 1963): 23.

3. [Monsieur Verdoux: Review], autograph manuscript/working draft, n.d., [c. May–June, 1947], University of Texas Library.

4. See Perry, pp. 54–138; Mayo, pp. 161–202.

5. Letter to [John Crowe] Ransom, autograph letter/draft/incomplete, n.d. [winter 1952?], University of Texas Library.

Chapter 1: Backward Beyond Remembrance

The biographical information in this chapter has been gleaned from reading two unpublished doctoral dissertations, which in turn were based on interviews with Agee's family and friends over a period from 1966 to 1968. See Concannon, pp. 1–5 and Mayo, pp. 1–30. Additional information was provided by my own interviews with Father James Harold Flye, Dwight Macdonald, and David McDowell in New York on December 28 and 29, 1970.

1. Joseph Wood Krutch, *More Lives Than One: An Autobiography* (New York, 1962), p. 5.

2. *Letters*, p. 172. Robert Fitzgerald, "Introduction," *Poems*, p. xi.

3. The Bell Tower of Amiens," *Phillips Exeter Monthly* 30 (December 1925):48–51; "The Scar," *PEM* 30 (January 1926): 77–78; "Beauvais," *PEM* 30 (May 1926), 177.

4. "Jenkinsville," *PEM* 30 (December 1926): 71. For the preceeding, cf. "Elmer Gantry," *PEM* 31 (May 1927): 189–91; "Knoxton High," *PEM* 31 (April 1927): 161–66.

5. "Between Trains," *PEM* 31 (May 1927): 171–73; "Sentimental Journey," *PEM* 32 (March 1928): 133–37; "Bound for the Promised Land," *PEM* 32 (January 1928): 85–88; "Chivalry An Allegory," *PEM* 32 (November 1927): 25–40.

6. "Between Trains," p. 171; "The Battler," *In Our Time* (New York, 1958), p. 65.

7. "Minerva Farmer," *PEM* 30 (November 1925); 39–42; "Sacre du Printemps," *PEM* 32 (April 1928): 158–60.

8. See Ohlin, *passim.* Ohlin's views have prevailed almost without qualification for every reader following him, excepting J. Douglas Perry.

9. "Pygmalion" [Poem], Typed carbon copy manuscript, [4pp], n.d. [c. December 1927–May 1928], University of Texas Library.

10. "Inquest on Democracy," *Time* 39 (June 15, 1942): 84.

11. "Roan Stallion," in *The Selected Poetry of Robinson Jeffers* (New York, 1959), pp. 141–57.

12. "Anne Garner," *PEM*, 32 (May 1928): 178.

13. "Reflections on *Permit Me Voyage*," Typed manuscript, n.d. collated with "The Poems of James Agee and related documents," edited and with a memoir by Robert Fitzgerald, 1964, University of Texas Library. Interestingly, Fitzgerald notes in *Prose*, p. 24, that Agee was close to death during the tonsillectomy as a result of hemophilia(?)

14. Most readers have suggested only two other possible influences for "Anne Garner": E. A. Robinson and Robert Frost. Agee discounts the Robinson influence in his May 1929 letter to Macdonald. He also indicates that he did not think highly of Frost at the time. See his pointed remarks in "John Carter," *Poems*, p. 90, on Robinson, Frost, Eliot, and Jeffers.

Chapter 2 - A Portrait of the Artist as a Young Man

A standard treatment of aestheticism is Edmund Wilson's *Axel's Castle: A Study in the Literary Imagination of 1870–1930* (New York, 1931); see also Malcolm Cowley, "The Death of Dada," in *Exile's Return, A Literary Odyssey of the 1920's* (New York, 1951), pp. 138–70. For further comments which have shaped my thinking, see Lionel Trilling, "Reality in America," in *The Liberal Imagination* (New York, 1950), pp. 3–21; Benjamin de Mott, "In and Out of Universal City: Reflections on the New Journalism and the Old Fiction," *Antioch Review* 29 (spring 1969): 15–24; Philip Rahv, "Notes on the Decline of Naturalism," in *Critiques and Essays in Modern Fiction, 1920–1951*, ed. John W. Aldridge (New York, 1952), pp. 415–23; William Wiegand, "The Non-Fiction Novel," *New Mexico Quarterly* 37 (autumn 1967): 243–57.

1. For Keats' definition of the vale of Soul-making," see his letter to George and Georgiana Keats, Sunday 14 Feb.–Monday 3 May 1819, in *Selected Poetry and Letters*, ed. Richard Fogle

(New York, 1960), pp. 325-31; for that of "Negative Capability," see the Letter to George and Thomas Keats, Sunday [21 Dec. 1817], pp. 303-05. The two quotations which follow are taken from the former, pp. 329, 330, respectively.

2. The relationship between "Epithalamium" and "Anne Garner" and Agee's later prose is analysed perceptively by Perry, pp. 18-35.

3. I. A. Richards, *Science and Poetry* (London, 1926), p. 20. See Robert Fitzgerald's comments on Richards in "Memoir," pp. 12-14, 17, 30-31.

4. *The Poetical Works of Wordsworth*, ed. Thomas Hutchinson, Second Edition revised by Ernest de Selincourt (London, 1964), p. 735.

5. See Durrant Da Ponte, "James Agee: The Quest for Identity," *Tennessee Studies in Literature* 8 (1963): 29; Robert Bingham, "Short of a Distant Goal," *Reporter* 27 (October 25, 1962): 56; Anonymous, "The Unquiet One," *Time* 80 (August 3, 1962): 60; and John Updike, "No Use Talking," *The New Republic,* 147 (August 13, 1963): 24.

Chapter 3 - Depression 1932-1935

1. "At a certain clearly definable moment . . . ." autograph manuscript/working draft/fragments, [4 pp], n.d. University of Texas Library.

2. "The Non-Fiction Novel," *The New Mexico Quarterly* 37 (autumn 1967): 243-57.

3. See L. S. Dembo, "Hart Crane's 'Verticalist' Poem," *American Literature* 40 (March 1968): 77-81. Agee gave verticalism more than passing notice. The poem "Lyric—a Song" (*Poems*, p. 153), published in *transition* 24 (June, 1936): 7, was

published in *The Saturday Review of Literature* 14 (September 5, 1936): 9, under the title "Vertigral."

4. See Ohlin, pp. 12–48, Behar, pp. 11–33, Concannon, pp. 43–98, Kramer, pp. 12–35, Perry, pp. 12–52.

5. See William Rose Benet, "The Phoenix Nest," *The Saturday Review of Literature* 11 (November 24, 1934): 314; Florence Codman, Review of *Permit Me Voyage, The Nation* 140 (January 23, 1935): 109; Babette Deutsch, Review of *Permit Me Voyage, Survey Graphic* 24 (March 1935): 135; Horace Gregory, "The Beginning of Wisdom," *Poetry* 46 (April 1935): 48–51; P. C. G., Review of *Permit Me Voyage, The New York Times* (December 30, 1934): 10; Lincoln Kirstein, "First Poems," *The New Republic* 82 (February 27, 1935): 80–81; David McCord, Review of *Permit Me Voyage, Yale Reviews,* n.s. 4 (winter 1935): 394; Theodore Morrison, Review of *Permit Me Voyage, Atlantic Bookshelf* 155 (March 1935): 12; and E. L. Walton, Review of *Permit Me Voyage,* New York *Herald Tribune* Book Review (December 9, 1934): 19.

6. See Perry, especially pp. 4–5, 42–50, 81–83, 139, and passim.

7. *transition* 26 (fall 1937): 7. The poem was originally printed in the format of a prose paragraph. Fitzgerald has altered it to fit metered lines. See *Poems,* pp. 59–60.

8. *Directions in Modern Poetry* (New York, 1940), p. 247.

9. See "Before God and this company; or Bigger than we are," [story], autograph manuscript/incomplete, n.d. [5 pp], University of Texas Library.

10. Incorporated in *A Death in the Family*. The piece was published in a slightly different form in *Partisan Review* 5 (August–September 1938): 22–25.

Chapter 4 - A Way of Seeing.

1. *Memoirs of a Revolutionist* (New York, 1957), p. 8.

2. "James Agee: *Let Us Now Praise Famous Men,*" in *Landmarks in American Writing,* ed. Henig Cohen (New York, 1969), p. 330.

3. "When you have apprehended that basket as one thing and have then analysed it according to its form and apprehended it as a thing you make the only synthesis which is logically and esthetically permissible. You see that it is that thing which it is and no other thing. The radiance of which he speaks is the scholastic *quidditas,* the *whatness* of a thing." James Joyce, *A Portrait of the Artist as a Young Man,* corr. Chester G. Anderson, ed. Richard Ellman (New York, 1967), p. 213. Dedalus' explanation in the draft, *Stephen Hero,* is more easily related to Agee: "This is the moment which I call epiphany. First we recognise that the object is *one* integral thing, then we recognise that it is an organised composite structure, a *thing* in fact: finally, when the relation of the parts is exquisite, when the parts are adjusted to the special point, we recognise that it is that thing which it is. Its soul, its whatness, leaps to us from the vestment of its appearance. The soul of the commonest object, the structure of which is so adjusted, seems to us radiant. The object achieves its epiphany." The quotation is taken from the edition by Theodore Spencer, incorporating additional manuscript pages, edited by John J. Slocum and Herbert Cahoon (New York, 1963), p. 213. See Hugh Kenner's "The School of Old Aquinas," in *Dublin's Joyce* (Boston, 1962), pp. 134–57, for a perceptive philosophic and literary analysis of Dedalus' *claritas* or radiance.

4. Erskine Caldwell and Margaret Bourke-White, *You Have Seen Their Faces* (New York, 1937); Dorothea Lange and Paul Schuster Taylor, *An American Exodus* (New York, 1939). In *Time* 35 (February 12, 1940): 80, Agee reviewed *American*

Exodus and criticized it for its "tear jerking inherent in dialect reused by sophisticates."

5. Anonymous, "Experiment in Communication," *Time* 38 (October 13, 1941): 104; C. Wright Mills, "Sociological Poetry," *Politics* 5 (spring 1948):125; John C. Cort, "Contemporary Social Problems," *Commonweal* 34 (September 12, 1941): 500; Ruth Lechlitner, "Alabama Tenant Families," New York *Herald Tribune* Book Review (August 24, 1941): 10; Selden Rodman, "The Poetry of Poverty," *Saturday Review* 24 (August 23, 1941): 4.

6. See "Sonnet V," *PMV*, p. 48, ll. 7–8, for the use of the same metaphor.

7. [Let Us Now Praise Famous Men:Notes], autograph manuscript/notebook, n.d., [c. 1940], University of Texas Library. Compare to I. A. Richards' language in *Principles of Literary Criticism* (London, 1934), pp. 261–64. Agee wrote, both in the notebook and in his preface (pp. xv–xvi), that "the reader is no less essential a center of our subject than ourselves and those we tell of; and to no less responsible," and that he and Evans were "observers awaiting new contributions to their subject"; they invited "those who wish actively to participate in the subject . . . to address the authors in care of the publishers." In August 1939, Agee had written Father Flye that he might work for Harper's (then publishers of *Famous Men*) on an edition of letters "the mutual property of three" and asked if some of Flye's letters could be used (*Letters*, p. 118). It seems reasonable to assume that the shape of the projected second volume would have been such a collection of letters from the tenants, the authors, and the readers.

8. See Ohlin, pp. 58–65, and Kramer, pp. 40–51, for a thorough analysis of the four planes.

9. *A Way of Seeing* (New York, 1965), p. 4.

10. [A Way of Seeing] autograph manuscript/working draft, n.d. [c. 1940], University of Texas Library.

11. [Let Us Now Praise Famous Men] , typed manuscript/incomplete [26 pp.], n.d., [c. 1940–41], University of Texas Library, "p. 354." Also, see Ohlin, pp. 58–65 for his analysis of the book as a five-movement symphony.

12. See Morris W. Croll, "The Baroque Style in Prose," reprinted from *Studies in English Philology: A Miscellany in Honor of Frederick Klaeber,* eds. Kemp Malone and Martin B. Ruud (Minneapolis, 1929), in *Seventeenth-Century Prose and Poetry,* eds. Alexander M. Witherspoon and Frank J. Warnke, Second Edition (New York, 1963), pp. 1065–77.

13. *American Renaissance* (New York, 1964), p. 30.

14. *Selected Prose and Poetry,* ed. Reginald L. Cook (New York, 1960), p. 15.

15. "Inquest on Democracy," *Time* 39 (June 15, 1942): 85.

16. "James Agee—The Question of Wasted Talent," in *The Novel of Violence in America,* (Dallas, Texas, 1957). p. 219.

17. Dwight Macdonald, "After Seven Years. 1. A Way of Death," *Politics* 5 (spring 1948): 124; Lionel Trilling, "Greatness with One Fault in It," *Kenyon Review* 4 (winter 1942): 102.

18. "Let Us Now Praise Famous Men," typed and typed carbon copy manuscript/incomplete with autograph corrections and autograph list of chapters, [283 pp.], n.d., [1939?], University of Texas Library. The Library has recently acquired this manuscript, which had been in Walker Evans' possession.

19. [Let Us Now Praise Famous Men: Notes]. See "Plans for Work: October 1937," *Prose,* pp. 147–66, and [Let Us Now Praise Famous Men:Notes], and "Notes and Suggestions on the magazine under discussion," typed carbon copy manuscript, [8 pp.], n.d., [1942?], University of Texas Library.

20. *A Way of Seeing* and "Notes on a portfolio of photographs by Walker Evans," *The Cambridge Review* 5 (1956): 25.

Chapter 5 - Epiphany and Dream

1. Mayo, p. 169; from an interview with Mrs. Agee in New York, May 29, 1968.

2. "Portrait of an Artist," *Time* 25 (February 19, 1940): 86.

3. *Stephen Hero*, p. 213.

4. "The School of Old Aquinas," *Dublin's Joyce* p. 152.

5. See Agee's notes for *Grapes of Wrath* in [*Famous Men: Notes*]; *Reviews*, p. 31, for *The Human Comedy*; pp. 166–69 for *The Southerner*.

6. See also "In an extremely interesting article in the current issue of *Chimera*. . ." autograph manuscript, [3 pp], n.d. [c. 1945], University of Texas Library.

7. [Monsieur Verdoux: Review], autograph manuscript/working draft, n.d., [c. May–June, 1947], University of Texas Library.

8. Typed carbon copy letter and notes to "Archie" [MacLeish], [20 pp], August 6, [1944?], University of Texas Library.

9. See Sidney Hook, "The New Failure of Nerve," *Partisan Review* 10 (January–February 1942): 2–23; Philip Wheelwright, "Dogmatism—New Style," *Chimera* 1 (spring 1943): 7–16.

10. "Marx, I agree. . . " typed manuscript, n.d., University of Texas Library.

11. "November 1945," typed carbon copy with autograph emendations, n.d., [November 1945], University of Texas Library. The poem has been published in "Agee in the Forties: Unpublished Poetry and Fiction by James Agee," *The Texas Quarterly* 11 (spring 1968): 18–19.

12. "Poor child . . .," catalogued with "If in that darkness where still a little while," autograph manuscript/working draft with autograph emendations, n.d., University of Texas Library.

13. [Christmas, 1945], autograph manuscript/working draft, n.d., [c. October–December, 1945], University of Texas Library. The published version can be found under the same title in *Time*, 46 (December 24, 1945), 56.

Chapter 6 - Directive.

1. [unidentified fragment: "Bomb"], autograph manuscript, n.d., [August, 1945], University of Texas Library.

2. The incident was related to me by Father Flye in conversation, December 28, 1970.

3. Father Flye thinks the novel to which Agee is referring in his November, 1945 letter is *The Morning Watch*. However, Agee wrote to Father Flye on May 23, 1950 (*Letters*, p. 181), that he has just finished the first draft "of the story about Maundy Thursday." It seems unlikely that it took him five years to complete a first draft for such a short piece. Agee had written three story outlines for films, variations of the Petrushka story, specifically dealing with adolescent love, all set in the 1920's. See [unidentified story: outlines and notes], autograph manuscript with autograph emendations, [13 pp on 6 ll.], n.d. [1946–48], University of Texas Library. The opening of the second sketch and setting of the third are identical with the unfinished manuscript discussed below, dating from the mid-1940s and entitled "1928 Story." See Kramer, pp. 128–46, and the published version in *The Texas Quarterly* 11 (spring 1968): 23–37. Very probably one of these is the manuscript to which he refers in the 1945 letter as "a short novel about adolescence in the 1920's." Needless to say, the importance of these interrelations is hardly bibliographical. Agee saw a real connection between the processes of conceptualizing and of writing fiction and film, which is one of the unforeseen results of his film criticism. Perhaps the missing link can be found in the manner in which he recreated important scenes from films and included them in his column. For other

film-fiction projects, see [unidentified play], autograph manuscript/incomplete, [7 pp], n.d., and [unidentified story: "All Through the night . . ."], autograph manuscript, [9 pp], n.d., University of Texas Library. The story is edited and appears in Kramer, pp. 147-60, under the title "Fragment of a Short

Story: Setting—Civil War." In an autograph memorandum to George Stevens, autograph manuscript/draft/incomplete, n.d. [c. 1952], University of Texas Library, Agee writes to the effect that he should show Stevens his "Civil War Story and: The 'Twilight' Story," as a possibility for films.

4. "American Apocalypse: Notes on the Bomb and The Failure of Imagination," in *The Forties: Fiction, Poetry, Drama*, ed. Warren French (Deland, Florida, 1969), pp. 141-51.

5. "Agrarianism and Politics," *Review of Politics* 1 (March 1939): 121.

6. "In an extremely interesting article in the current issue of *Chimera*. . .," autograph manuscript [3 pp], n.d. [1945], University of Texas Library.

7. [unidentified television script or screenplay], autograph manuscript/working draft with autograph revisions [62 pp], n.d. [c. 1947-48], University of Texas Library. The manuscript pages are not numbered. Hence, all future references are to this manuscript and are not noted in the text. A synopsis was published by Victor Kramer under the title "Agee in the Forties: The Struggle to be a Writer," in *The Texas Quarterly* 11 (spring 1968): 11-14.

8. See Wright Morris, "The Territory Ahead," in *Modern American Fiction*, ed. A. Walton Litz (New York, 1963), pp. 338-65; R. W. B. Lewis, *The American Adam* (Chicago, 1959).

9. [Monsieur Verdoux: Review], autograph manuscript/working draft, n.d. [May-June 1947], University of Texas Library.

10. See "Run Over" and "Give Him Air" in *Prose*, pp. 137-40,

and "Two Sonnets From a Dream," *Botteghe Oscure,* No. 5 (May 1950): 336-37.

11. In his letter dated March 2, 1948 (*Letters,* p. 170), Agee indicated that he began the novel in the fall of 1947 and worked on it intermittently from January to March 1948. In two letters, dated May 4, 1949, and May 23, 1950 (*Letters,* p. 179, 181), he indicates that he is going to spend the summer of 1949 at his Hillsdale farm and, in the second letter, that he had gotten "a lot done" at that time; also he speaks of getting ready to type the novel.

12. "James Agee," in *Against the American Grain,* p. 150.

13. [A Death in the Family: Notes and fragments], autograph manuscript [6 pp], n.d., University of Texas Library.

14. See Kenneth Curry's note in *Publications of the Bibliographical Society of America* 114 (First Quarter 1970): 84-98, and Kramer's own, more authoritative, "The Manuscript and the Text of James Agee's *A Death in the Family,*" which will appear in *PBSA.* Quoted from a xerox copy in possession of the author.

15. [A Death in the Family: Notes], autograph manuscript [20 pp], n.d. University of Texas Library.

16. [A Death in the Family: Notes and fragments].

17. "The Accidents of Compassion," *The Reporter* 17 (December 12, 1957): 43.

18. [A Death in the Family: Notes and fragments].

19. [The Morning Watch: pages of incomplete draft], n.d., University of Texas Library.

20. Victor Kramer's article, "James Agee's Unpublished Manuscript and his Emphasis on Religious Emotion in *The Morning Watch,*" will appear in *Tennessee Studies in Literature.* Xerox copy in possession of the author.

21. Sense and Sensibility," *Kenyon Review* 13 (autumn 1951): 689, 688.

22. *Against the American Grain,* p. 150.

23. "Character, Theme and Symbol in *The Morning Watch,*" *Western Humanities Review* 15 (autumn 1961): 359–67. See also Ohlin, pp. 187–94.

Chapter 7 - The Full Life is Full of Crap.

1. [Monsieur Verdoux: Review], autograph manuscript/working draft, n.d. [c. May–June, 1947], University of Texas Library.

2. "For several years I reviewed movies for *Time* and *The Nation* . . .," autograph manuscript, n.d., [1952?], University of Texas Library.

3. "The absolute fundamental, it is democratic . . .," autograph manuscript with autograph emendations [5 pp on 4 ll.], n.d., [1946], University of Texas Library.

4. " 'The Blue Hotel': An examination of Story and Film Script," *Film Heritage* 3 (fall 1967): 22–23 and passim.

5. [The Blue Hotel: Notes] autograph manuscript/notes [6 pp], n.d. [October 1950], University of Texas Library.

6. Of the seven writers who consider Agee's film work, Ohlin simply calls it a different category. Seib considers it the work of a frustrated writer. Perry sees it as a development toward the word. Behar, Synder, and Mayo are noncommittal. In my own dissertation I tried to indicate that I considered the scripts as hack work, a thesis I have obviously qualified in this writing.

7. Typed carbon copy letter to Fred [Zinneman], January 12, 1954, University of Texas Library, p. 32.

8. Typed carbon copy letter to David Bradley, Saturday, 26 June 53 [Saturday, June 27, 1953], University of Texas Library.

9. See Lillian Ross' interesting sketch of Agee applying literary techniques to the script of *The African Queen* in her book, *Picture* (New York, 1952), pp. 142–45.

10. C. S. Forester, *The African Queen* (New York, 1964).

11. [The African Queen], typed carbon copy manuscript/revisions [14 pp], January 16–27, 1951, University of Texas Library. See *Scripts,* p. 213, l. 7, for the approximate break-off point. The scene was not revised.

12. "On Chaplin, Verdoux and Agee," *Esquire* 113 (April 1965): 34. See also Bosley Crowther's review of *Agee on Film* in *American Scholar* 29 (summer 1960): 436, and Richard Griffith "Reflections and Images," *The New York Times Book Review* (November 16, 1958): 5, 38.

13. "The Blue Hotel"/First Draft—James Agee/Critical Analysis, typed manuscript, October 23, 1950, University of Texas Library.

14. [The African Queen] autograph manuscript/working draft/notes, [111 pp], n.d. [December 1950], University of Texas Library.

15. "Noa Noa: the story of Paul Gauguin; a screenplay," typed carbon copy manuscript/incomplete [53 pp], n.d. [1953], University of Texas Library.

16. [A Tanglewood Story: Outline], typed carbon copy manuscript/incomplete [105 pp], n.d. [1954], University of Texas Library, p. 96.

17. [A Tanglewood Story: Outline], typed carbon copy manuscript [64 pp], n.d. [1954], University of Texas Library, p. 62.

18. See [Mr. Lincoln]. The beginning and the end; a prologue, composite typed manuscript and typed manuscript/mimeo with autograph emendations [108 pp], n.d. [1952], University of Texas Library.

19. See Whittaker Chambers' moving portrait, "Agee," in *Cold Friday* (New York, 1964), p. 269.

20. Typed carbon copy letter to David Bradley, Monday 28 June, 1953 [Monday, June 29, 1953], University of Texas Library.

Credits   The author gratefully acknowledges the use and permission to quote from "James Agee by Himself," *Esquire* 60(December 1963); "Jenkinsville," *Phillips Exeter Monthly* 31(December 1926); "Menalcas," *PEM* 32(December 1927); "Anne Garner," *PEM* 32(May 1928); "Sheeps and Shuttleworths," *Fortune* 7(January 1933); "The Third Favorite Flavor," *Fortune* 7(April 1933); "The Project is Important," *Fortune* 8(October 1933); "Art For What's Sake?" *New Masses* 21(December 15, 1936); "Inquest on Democracy," *Time* 39(June 15, 1942); "Portrait of an Artist," *Time* 25(February 19, 1940); "Victory, the Peace: The Bomb," *Time* 46(August 20, 1945); "Democratic Vistas," *Time* 46(November 5, 1945); "Godless Gotterdämmerung," *Time* 46(October 15, 1945); "Religion and the Intellectuals," *The Partisan Review* 17(February 1950); the James Agee Papers at the University of Texas Library; the Letters of James Agee to Dwight Macdonald; "1928 Story" and "Dream Sequence," *The Texas Quarterly* 11(Spring 1968); *A Death in the Family* (New York, 1957; 1963); *Agee on Film: Reviews and Comments* (New York, 1958; Boston, 1964); and *Agee on Film: Five Film Scripts* (New York, 1958; Boston, 1964), c. The James Agee Trust.

He is also indebted to the Houghton Mifflin Company for the use and permission to quote from *The Collected Short Prose of James Agee,* ed. Robert Fitzgerald (Boston, 1969; New York, 1970); *The Collected Poems of James Agee,* ed. Robert Fitzgerald (Boston, 1969; New Haven, Conn. 1969); *The Letters of James Agee to Father Flye* (New York, 1962); *Let Us Now Praise Famous Men* (Boston, 1941; 1960); and *The Morning Watch* (Boston, 1950; New York, 1966).

Finally, the author wishes to acknowledge the use and permission to quote from "Roan Stallion" by Robinson Jeffers in *The Selected Poetry of Robinson Jeffers* (New York, 1959), © Random House, Inc., and from *A Way of Seeing: Photographs of New York* by Helen Levitt with an essay by James Agee (New York, 1965), © The Viking Press, Inc.